1

# A Christian Libertarian Looks at the Major Political Issues

*What Would Jesus Do?*

By Peter J Dellas, Ph.D
co-authored by Joyce Dellas

# Contents

3

# Preface

I started out writing this book because I have engaged many people over the years on political thought as it pertains to my Christian faith. The Facebook phenomenon has only served to make this an almost daily part of our lives.  How often do you get on Facebook to see anti-Obama or anti-Trump posts which usually become an argument of personalities over substance and policy?  This is where we are today in a divided America.

This book was meant to address the major political issues in the USA that we face today. Some of these issues go back many years. Others have come to the fore in recent times. As Christians, the core values that we have which help us to address these issues are unchanging. They should emanate from the New Testament upon the foundation that was built in the Old Testament. For believers, the New Testament is what guides us and the Old Testament simply gives us context. This is why we can eat shrimp, have no need to sacrifice lambs, and we worship on Sundays. Thank God that we are not under the law, but under grace.

I am not trying to be scholarly in this book. This is not a treatise or a dissertation of any sort. I am not trying to impress college professors or liberal intellectuals. I am intentionally writing in plain language and making plain arguments using my Christian faith and common sense as led by the Holy Spirit to guide me in my beliefs and arguments. It is my prayer that as you read this book, you keep that all in mind. I also pray that God uses this book in your life to help clarify some of the political issues that we face today. Being a Christian in these times is not an easy thing. Discrimination against our faith is not only everywhere, but seems to be encouraged by the left. There is an attack against Christian values that is no longer subtle. And what makes it more egregious is that many who call themselves "Christians" are also leading that attack. To a world of non-believers, this makes them think that there is something wrong with us. This makes them think that since they also have so-called "Christians" among them, it is our "type" of Christianity that must be flawed. This is often much more than can be dealt with in the context of political arguments. But I do address it in this book.

For those who are mature believers, who have read the Word and understand its message, who are filled with the Spirit and have a living relationship with Jesus, we can take comfort in the fact that, ultimately, we belong to Him. We are merely sojourners in this world, as ambassadors of His Kingdom, hoping to fairly represent to this world our king, Jesus. God bless you as you read.

Pete Dellas
Joyce Dellas

# Reconciling Libertarian Ideas with Christianity

Over the years some Christians have asked me how I reconcile my Christian faith with the positions of libertarianism. They point out that libertarians would allow gays to marry or would allow people to buy drugs or get abortions. They also point to Ayn Rand, a libertarian philosopher and playwright that helped formulate what is much of modern libertarianism, and how she was an atheist. I want to start out by addressing this supposed conflict.

I want to first clarify that I am not a member of the American Libertarian Party, nor do I believe that party represents true libertarian thinking. As I see it, libertarian thought has its roots in the Classical Liberalism of the 18th and 19th centuries and gave rise to the founding of the United States and its Declaration of Independence, Bill of Rights and Constitution. Much of what is called "American Conservatism" today is similar to this classical liberal thought. So as I use the word "libertarian" throughout this book, be aware that I am using it as a label for a set of ideas that are very compatible with Christianity, not as a political party.

I should also point out that conservatism today has a subgroup of followers who are neoconservatives. These people tend to believe in militarism and American foreign interventionism far more than I believe Christians should support. The two Bush presidencies, George Bush Sr. and George Bush Jr., exemplified this sort of neoconservative thinking. In both cases, they appealed to the United Nations for the legal cover to go to war in Iraq. In both cases I believe they were wrong. Christians should be very hesitant to engage in war at all. And if Christians are involved in any war, it should be in self-defense or for humanitarian reasons. I am very familiar with the arguments for Christian pacifism and I do not subscribe to them. Simply put, God gets no glory by allowing evil to flourish. In fact, in my view, ignoring the systematic rape and murder of people is consent for it to happen. I believe James 4:17 is clear on this point when he says "Therefore, to one who knows the right thing to do and does not do it, to him it is sin."

Libertarians believe in a free society. As a Christian, I see how the poor are abused for political gain and how they are conditioned by our entitlement society to become dependents and not care for themselves. Then I think of Paul's word to the Thessalonian Church "If a man will not work, he shall not eat." (II Thessalonians 3:10). I think of how our politicians are enslaving the poor only to offer them crumbs off the table. I think of how government takes from those who work to give it to those who do not work, effectively disincentivizing hard work. I think of how some make the calculation that working for a wage of $12 an hour is less profitable than collecting an unemployment check--which often means other government benefits are also there for them to exploit. Libertarians wouldn't continue to fund living off the government as a lifestyle choice. They would encourage free enterprise, which would create jobs and where people can work to make a living. Ronald Reagan once said that a Job is the best anti-poverty program. I couldn't agree more.

My Christian faith compels me to help to poor. Let's face it: Not all who receive entitlements are lazy. But many are, and game the system to make a lifestyle choice of living off the sweat of others. Just as my faith compels me to help the poor, it also looks at the slothful and lazy with disdain. "Slothfulness casts into a deep sleep; and an idle soul shall suffer hunger" (Proverbs 19:15). Laziness brings people to bondage. Sometimes that bondage is not traditional slavery but the bondage of government--being trapped and no longer free because of the dependence you have on them for your basic needs. "Work hard and become a leader; be lazy and become a slave." (Proverbs 12:24).

The libertarian argument about homosexual marriage is a relatively simple one. If government controls marriage, theoretically it can ban homosexual marriage. But we have seen how that plays out with politicians. Bill Clinton signed the Defense of Marriage Act ( D.O.M.A.) and "Don't ask, don't tell"--both of which were abandoned under the Obama administration. So how well did that work out? And then the Supreme Court ruled on gay marriage, too, and gave it the status of a civil right. We saw that they did this with abortion as well. Reading the decisions on those two issues is like reading fanciful sophistry. Abortion was tied to a "right to privacy" which is a vague reference to the fourth amendment. And Obergefell decision, which gives the right for gays to marry, was written by Justice Anthony Kennedy and made out of whole cloth from sociological arguments.

Furthermore, when the government controls marriage, any group can get a protected status. This has meant that your kids will learn about gay lifestyles in school because the government wishes to mainstream gay marriage to "promote tolerance." The homeowner who lives in half a duplex will be forced to let a gay couple rent the other half even if he doesn't want to expose his young kids to that lifestyle. It will be a civil rights issue which will always trump any property rights or religious objections—especially because religion has now been unofficially relegated to a classification of intolerance, unless (of course) it is Islam. Islam is somehow seen as worthy of defense.

However, all of that goes away if government stays out of marriage. Fringe churches and rebellious pastors will still marry gays. But nobody will be forced to recognize them. We will be free to accept or reject them based on the dictates of our faith or our conscience. This seems to answer the question of their "right to marry" while also answering a Christian's right to not associate with an openly gay lifestyle. I'm not in any way advocating hate. I am advocating liberty. We are all sinners and all need to be saved by grace. That includes homosexuals. That includes heterosexuals.

On the illegal drugs issue, this is more a matter of reducing violence and corruption than anything else. People doing drugs are already messing up their lives. The government adds another layer to that--the layer of violence. Any "black market" is created when a government controls certain trade. Guns, drugs, alcohol, etc have all been controlled and have resulted in past or present black markets. Stop creating a black market for drugs and the violence will mostly stop. The analogy of Prohibition is real. The Saint Valentine's Day Massacres stopped after prohibition was lifted. Nobody stands in a dark ally anymore offering to sell you black market beer. Maybe it is not a perfect analogy. But history shows us that black markets create violence.

This is really a lesson of basic economics. The Bible says that "the love of money is the root of ALL evil" (I Timothy 6:10). Well, here is evidence. What makes the drug trade so lucrative is the fact that they are illegal. That means that the illegal drug trade can be lucrative because of the great efforts it takes to evade interdiction and law enforcement efforts in order to deliver them. But what that also means is that the delivery process is treacherous. People are getting killed every day and violence is a very real part of this underground economy. In fact, most of the gun violence that we see in society today comes from the illegal drug trade. And it is indiscriminate in the way that innocent people, guilty people, law enforcement, and even little kids all get caught in the crossfire of this drug trade. All of this is the direct result of these drugs being illegal. There's lots of money to be made and people will kill for it.

What about abortion? Some of my Libertarian Party friends may disagree with me, but I believe abortion is the taking of a human life and should therefore be adjudicated that way. I believe a true libertarian minded judge would see that protecting the life of the least among us would cause him to find abortion illegal in most cases. But, even if they don't, a libertarian defunding of groups like Planned Parenthood would decrease abortions significantly. They are the chief abortion mills in the country. It would leave abortions to those who can afford them instead of making you and me pay for them. Some will say that the tax dollars we send Planned Parenthood are not supposed to pay for abortions. That's like saying the money in your left pocket can't be spent for bills, only the money in your right pocket. Do you believe that? By funding Planned Parenthood's "other" works, it frees up the rest of their money to go 100% toward abortion. We aren't stupid. That is Washington DC logic and it is for the gullible.

And libertarians believe that we shouldn't be in wars unless our country is directly threatened. What would Jesus say about that? I think it is obvious that libertarian thinking on this point is closer to Christianity than either of the two parties today. It turns out that as a matter of history that Democrats have gotten the USA in almost all of our foreign wars. The exception to that is the two Bushes, George Sr. and George Jr., who acted less like true conservatives and more like "progressives." It is the reason we have to distinguish between "conservatives" and "neocons" who may share many conservative positions but also tend to favor military use far more than a true conservative.

So how is an ideology of libertarianism compatible with true historic Christianity? My answer is simple: Christianity is a free-willed faith. There is no compulsion in Christianity, as much as some believe that Calvin's theories of predestination are gospel. A free society is far better than one where government power and coercion tries to effect outcomes. Real Christians aren't born into Christian families or baptized into the faith as infants or declared Christians by the society that they live in. Real Christians make a faith decision to accept Jesus as their Lord and Savior and become born again by the Spirit of God as a result. It is because many do not know this that there is general confusion between nominal Christianity--that is, those who are Christians in name only—and true Christians who have placed their faith in Christ by their own choice and volition.

Are you really free?

Think about that question because it is evident that we aren't. When the government can cause you to conform to their way of thinking, and get you to behave the way the political class wants you to, and bring you to live within the parameters they have set up, and eat the foods they suggest, and believe the way they want you to believe, you are under their control. You are not a free agent, but a drone. You serve the collective, but the collective serves the queen bee. You are a brick in the wall. A cog in the machine. A disposable and replaceable proletarian serving the perpetuation of the political bourgeoisie. You're merely a prole, a peasant, a serf--serving the new lords of the government manor. The political aristocracy ascertains that you will serve their needs, forging your chains and shackles by the numerous laws they impose on you to keep their status, and yours.

This is a kinder, gentler form of slavery. The slaves were fed portions of their labors and you are as well. The difference is that yours are converted to paper (dollars) to give the semblance of freedom. But they control those dollars. You are only free to move around within the fenced area--the parameters they have defined for you. Your choices are limited by the masters. They define your liberty. The menu is limited. And modern liberals are willing enforcers of this slavery by silencing those who would oppose it with threats of riot. Is this still the USA?

The major purpose of government is to secure our God-given rights of life, liberty, property, and the pursuit of happiness. All laws essentially ought to boil down to that. So, when the government begins to prey upon the people, or begins to diminish people's liberty, takes people's property, or robs people's happiness, that government starts losing its legitimacy. That government is overstepping the bounds that were set upon it by the Founders. The powers of government were limited and enumerated in the Constitution but today's government has overstepped those powers and has gone beyond what was intended by the Founders.

Those citizens who will vote to preserve and even expand this current bloated and overreaching government actually vote for the slow creep of tyranny that we are currently under. This is not a Republican or Democrat thing. This is simply where the American government is today and has been progressing further away from liberty. This is why President Trump's deregulation orders early in his administration, his executive reviews, repeals, etc. were a welcome change to those who value liberty. Liberals ought to have also welcomed it. Instead they were fighting it every step of the way.

Both parties have had their part in getting us here. Both parties are at fault. The only solution will be either a collapse and anarchy followed by revolution, or a slow reversal of the creep in the hands of a smaller government president who will be held accountable by real metrics, not government propaganda. The transition to liberty will not be painless. But we owe it to our kids. In recent times there have been no elected Democrats who favor smaller government and many of the Republicans will only maintain the status quo or also increase the size and scope of government. That is where it stands.

Today's government pays no attention to Constitutional limits and has, rather, become a ubiquitous part of the People's lives. It is a hard, cold fact that liberty and tyranny cannot coexist--one must give way to the other. Today's government is taking on the characteristics historically associated with past tyrannies. The very "...repeated injuries and usurpations, all having in direct object the establishment of an absolute Tyranny..." that the Declaration of Independence listed have all been revisited upon the People. History tells us that these things usually do not end well.

For the sake of our posterity--the children and grandchildren that we say we love--we need to do what we can to curtail this intrusion into our lives before it ends ugly. It will matter little who wins the next World Series, or the next Superbowl, if in the coming years we are a nation in ruins--economic chains, social chaos, insecure in our life and property, unable to plan for the future, subject to do other people's wills.

17

# The Trump Phenomenon

During the 2016 election cycle, many Evangelicals asked how they can support a guy like Trump. I want to address that question because I believe it is a sincere one and deserves a detailed explanation. But first, I want to state that I hesitate to call myself an Evangelical anymore because that term now includes people who are pro-abortion, socialists, morally spineless, and even hold to least common denominator "faithism", churchianity, etc. So I am returning to where I started. I am a Fundamentalist Christian. Don't load that phrase with presuppositions that it doesn't contain. What it very simply means is that I believe the fundamentals of the Christian faith. I think most Christians prefer to be defined that way. The term "fundamentalist" took on some political baggage back in the 1980's and many abandoned it then. But I believe it is good to bring it back. A true Christian would simply want to do what Jesus would do. Not what we think He would do, but what He would actually do based on what He did in the New Testament. Deeds, not simply words.

I believe that the real spiritual crisis that Christianity faces today is the wishy-washy stance "Evangelicals" have taken on issues of clear biblical morality. I have no power over what Trump, Obama, Bush, Clinton or Reagan do in their personal lives. But as presidents they had/have the power to affect outcomes that are of concern to Christians. The real theological question we ought to be asking is "What do I care if God uses a murderer or a saint to accomplish His will?" As Christians, we believe that the Holy Spirit moves people to do His will. Regardless, my prayer is "Thy will be done on earth as it is in heaven." David and Moses were both murderers. And Moses wasn't particularly spiritual when God called him. He was a fugitive of murder.  This is why we pray for our country and our leaders if we are following what the New Testament teaches.

So the question I would ask is whether God can use a murderer, a blasphemer, a womanizer, or whatever to do His will? Why are we holding Trump to a standard that God has not held? If there is someone undignified and petulant, but who says he will do what is right and states his platform, isn't that better than the "dignified person" who has a platform that is wrong and anti-Christian?  Are the positions that Trump has taken better or worse than the positions that Obama had taken? Let's be honest because I think many Evangelicals are confused about this very thing. And, in case you aren't sure, I'll state here clearly that Obama's positions and policies were very anti-Christian and anti-biblical. His smooth demeanor caused people to think he was acting as a Christian. But it is his policies, not his demeanor and suave ways that should determine how he affected Christians.

The word "Evangelical" used to be a noble one and there was a time that I wore that badge with pride. Personally, I used to be affiliated with the Evangelical Free Church and served as a deacon for a few years and as pastor in one for a year. But in the 30 years that have since passed the term has lost its meaning. My faith and understanding of the Scriptures have only increased since then. And today it seems that many of those who identify as Evangelicals have lost their saltiness (i.e., Matthew 5:13). Maybe it's because politics is bastardizing religion. I think there are certain social issues that the Bible takes a clear position about such as homosexuality, abortion, transgenderism, etc. Some so-called "Evangelicals" have taken positions that are contrary to the Scriptures concerning these issues and it is because of them that I had to abandon that label for myself. Love the sinner, yes. But if you make him believe that his sin is OK, you have done nothing but deceive him. You are lying to him and that is not OK.

For me, it is as clear as II Corinthians 6:14-16:

"Do not be yoked together with unbelievers. For what do righteousness and wickedness have in common? Or what fellowship can light have with darkness? What harmony is there between Christ and Belial? Or what does a believer have in common with an unbeliever? What agreement is there between the temple of God and idols?"

The word "yoked" in that passage described a means to get two animals partnered to get some work done together. It is not simply being a friend. So what Paul says here is that we Christians shouldn't be entering into partnerships with unbelievers. I think this would mean businesses, indentures, investments, etc or even political. Maybe I am being too strict with this. But I left the Republican party a couple of years after George Bush got us involved in Iraq. I should have left when his father got us involved. But I was young and naive. I can't be yoked together with them. And now I no longer wish to identify as an Evangelical because that word has become politicized, too.

The Biblical stances taken on the social issues by the Democrat Party made it a non-option for me as a believer. Democrats have historically had a lot of good ideas, too, as did Republicans. And I saw the good in both parties. But I eventually realized that I shouldn't be identified with either. I can support an individual man who is a politician. In fact, I have several friends who are politicians, great men of God who love the Lord and who also happen to be elected officials. But I will not serve a party or be affiliated with one again.

Because of this, Evangelicalism now is almost a meaningless word to most Americans. It has become so politicized that it carries baggage I don't want to be associated with. Some are Democrats. Many are Republicans. Some are pro-abortion. Others are anti. Some are for gay marriage. Others are against it, etc. So I am not one of the "Evangelical vote."

The Founders had wisdom in trying to maintain a secular state. Don't let that statement get under your skin. I am not saying an irreligious state and I will explain this further throughout this book. But we need to know that the Founders were students of history and the blending of Christianity with politics is where we get into trouble—as if the government and the Kingdom of God are the same thing. They aren't and never should be confused! The government and the Kingdom of God are actually rivals. Our kingdom as Christians is the Kingdom of God. The government is a kingdom of this world, and those kingdoms will one day become the Lord's (Revelation 11:15). But they are not His today. In fact, they are under the domain of Satan (Luke 4:5-6). This present age is being rules by him, the "god of this age" (II Corinthians 4:4). In fact Jesus called Satan "the ruler of this world" in John's gospel several times (John 12:31, 14:30, 16:11).

Now, I want you to think about something else. I voted for Mitt Romney in 2012. What do you think? When I voted for a Mormon named Mitt Romney in 2012, did that mean I believed in the Mormon ideas of Kolob? Or in the Mormon angel Moroni? No, I don't. But I believed he would have done more than Barack Obama to resolve issues that can only be resolved by government power. I think many Christians have often confused the Kingdom of God with politics. In the Book of Isaiah, God called Cyrus--a heathen, murderous, king--"His anointed." In the Book of Romans, God called Pharaoh "elect" for His purpose to show His power and glory. In the Book of Exodus, God called Moses to free the Jews--an idolatrous, murderer who was raised by the persecutors of the Jews, the Egyptian Pharaohs. Moses didn't seek God. God sought him.

So, we really do have a spiritual problem because we are anemic as the church of Jesus Christ and because we have held our politicians to moral standards that continuously take our focus off the issues that are within their God-given purview (i.e., government, "the powers that be" Romans 13:1f). Put it another way, I'd vote an anti-abortion, anti-poverty capitalist, pro-freedom heathen, over a so-called "Christian" who was pro-abortion, who imposed the gay agenda on Christians, who sowed confusion in the schools concerning the immutability of the sexes (i.e., the whole transgenderism thing) etc. That was what Barack Obama in fact did, was it not?

Let me give you a historic illustration. Think back to the election of Jimmy Carter and Ronald Reagan in 1980. Ronald Reagan wasn't known at that time for his Christianity. He only spoke about "God" affectionately in the old school tradition of many politicians. I didn't know his heart and neither did you. Yet he turned out to do much that Christians can appreciate today. On the other hand, Jimmy Carter was a born-again Christian, Sunday School teacher and deacon in his church from Plains, Georgia in the heart of the Bible belt. By that point we'd had four years of him and saw that, though he may have been a nice guy, he wasn't a leader.

So this is where I am today. Thoroughly disgusted with the state of so-called "Christianity" and the poor testimony of what is called Christian in the world today. What kind of witness have we been to the world? The world has set the agenda and many so-called "Christians" are simply following it. You can't name the Name of Jesus and fellowship with immorality. There's a spiritual conflict there.

But I want to ask a theological question of my Christian friends: Thinking on the Old Testament story in Genesis, if God destroyed Sodom or if He saved it, wouldn't He still be the sovereign God? (Recall that both were options when He spoke with Abraham.) Some people have said that the USA is toast and God has sovereignly appointed it to judgment. They have given up on voting and have mostly ignored what is going on in the country. But I say that God's sovereignty is not what is at issue here. We are not fatalists. It is the people's will that is at issue. And God will act based on their will. Whatever "is" is not necessarily what is "right." We have the power to move mountains (Matthew 21:21). Jesus said that, not me. In other words, if we are simply complacent in the evil that we see, then we will be judged for our complacency. James comes to mind again when he said "To him who knows the right thing to do, and does it not, to him it is sin," James 4:17. Aren't we supposed to be the light of the world and the salt of the earth? What does that even mean if we allow darkness to prevail around us? If we let that happen, in what way are we then light? The light of the gospel is life-changing. It doesn't only transform a man's heart, but his life—his actions, his deeds, his choices, his values.

To illustrate this further, think about another story in the Old Testament, the great City of Nineveh which is near Mosul in modern-day Iraq. It was slated for destruction and the Prophet Jonah was sent there to preach its destruction (the Old Testament Book of Jonah). God made a spectacular effort to make sure that message of impending destruction was preached which took Jonah through the belly of the "whale" (i.e., a great fish) to make sure Jonah showed up for his appointed task. The overlying message being imparted there is that God was not kidding. (I am not going to argue whether this is to be taken allegorically or literally because it doesn't matter to this point I am making. But I will say that if you don't believe in the miraculous, you are not a Christian.)

Yet, after Jonah preached the destruction of that city, God saw the repentance of the people--their response to Jonah's message-- and He saved that city. God sovereignly *both* planned its destruction *and* relented from carrying it out based on the people's response. Why? Because God has appointed our free willed responses as the basis upon which He acts. Doesn't Christianity teach that people freely choose Jesus or Hell, and that God will eternally honor that choice? Someone once said "Eternity: Smoking or non-smoking? Which will you choose?"

Similarly, God will honor our desire to see this nation's moral backslide stop. He knows whether we are acting simply out of a desire for political power, or whether we are genuinely wanting to see truth, equity, the cessation of the abortion holocaust, the defense of the poor, the end of gender confusion politics, the seeking of righteousness, etc. I believe that, as Christians, those who supported the election of Trump are doing so believing God will do a work through a very flawed and broken vessel. And some of those Christians who didn't or couldn't support Trump were using their own [self] righteousness as the standard--which they will say is actually "holiness"-- and they are looking with disdain at Trump and saying, "God, I thank you that I am not like other people—robbers, evildoers, adulterers—or even like this tax collector. I fast twice a week and give a tenth of all I get," (Luke 18:10-11). Think about it because self-righteousness is certainly one of the biggest sins Jesus fought against with the Pharisees.

So, I ask you what Jesus asked there in that same Luke 18 passage: Which one was justified? Which one was truly looking to God to do a work in his life, as opposed to pointing to his own works? Which one self-righteously refuses to eat with the gentiles (i.e., Peter vs Paul in Galatians 2:11-14)? So, I am asking whether we are going to act as Christians in truth, or simply play the "holier than thou" game? I am not afraid to engage the world because I know the promise made to me is "the gates of hell shall not prevail against" me (Matthew 16:18). That verse is offense, brethren, not defense. I am the one beating down those gates and they cannot withstand me. That is not arrogance.  That is confidence in the One who's made the promise.

Rejecting Trump was an easy mistake to make because he was a flamboyant, belligerent and crude candidate. But realize that God uses such people and move forward, brethren. God is the One that has set up this man as president in response to the cries of His people. God sets up all authority on earth and

the people get what they allow. This means
that sometimes we get a president who
opposes God. Other times we get one who
doesn't. And neither (or both) might even call
themselves "Christians." Again, compare
Reagan and Carter.


Think on it.

So let's get something straight here. I am a
libertarian politically. But I will vote for the
person who has the best chance of advancing
my Christian libertarian views. Though that
tends to be a Republican, it is not always. And
I will tell you here that there is rarely a ballot
that I completely fill out. Very often I leave
spaces blank, intentionally, because the
candidate doesn't represent positions that I
can agree with as a Christian. Not his
character, nor his personality, but his *positions*.

Now, consider the history of politics as it
relates to this. Since the very beginning, the
Democrat Party has always exploited divisions
in our country. Democrats were the racists,
KKK, Jim Crow, anti-women's suffrage, etc.
party. They saw differences in people and used
those differences to unite a majority coalition
of racists since the early years of that party.
Then, sometime after the Kennedy election,
they saw that it was to their advantage to
exploit those same differences by embracing a
plurality of groups and build a majority that

way--just like they did after women gained the right to vote in 1920. Lyndon Johnson's legacy is really that very idea after he signed the Civil Rights Act of 1964. Politically, it is called "pivoting", and Democrats do it well. The Democrat Party is primarily a party of hyphenated-Americans today. We must not forget our history or we will repeat the mistakes we ought to have learned from.

And the people are not stupid. A Rasmussen poll conducted in August 2017 found that 72% of respondents believed that politicians exploit race for political purposes. They don't talk about race because they are genuinely concerned about racial issues. This poll is consistent with what we see all the time. How many Democrats actually sponsor legislation to deal with any of their racial concerns? Few if any because racism is not a genuine concern, it's instead an issue to manipulate a portion of the electorate. I must confess the Republicans do the same thing with abortion. How often do you get legislation from a Republican who make have run on his pro-life stance? Almost never. And even when they do, it is window dressing, not substantive.

Philosophically, Republicans have always been a party of equality. They do not pander to Blacks, Hispanics, gays, or any other group to gain their vote. Republicans have always believed that "all men are created equal and are endowed by their Creator in certain inalienable rights..." That is why after the Civil War, the Blacks who took office were all Republicans. They don't believe in special rights, reparations, affirmative action or any other government fix--which often have unintended consequences. They believe in equality for all, regardless of color, gender, race, ethnicity etc. They believe that government fixes and the coercion of the law will not compensate for simple equality. You don't fix racism with more racism.  Yet, when a Black person is known as a Republican, he is hated by Democrats and liberals because he refuses to play the race game.

To the extent that a Republican (or even a Democrat) supports the equality of all people, the limitation of government to the Enumerated Powers, *real* liberty and *true* justice, I will support that person. History is not just a bunch of facts. There are reasons why certain things happened and any student of history doesn't only ask WHO, WHAT, WHEN and WHERE, but also WHY and HOW doesn't get the whole story. And, as Christians, we cannot allow anyone to cause us to betray the fact that God is no respecter of persons and that there is no "Jew nor Gentile, neither slave nor free, nor is there male and female, for you are all one in Christ Jesus" (Galatians 3:28). If Paul were around today, I am quite sure he'd include "White or Black" in that verse because that is the Christian view on race as well.

# Abortion

The issue of abortion is one of the most heated in politics. And politicians have made it so that the First amendment is already in a shambles because of a liberal redefinition of religion. Now, you cannot practice your faith except within the confines of a building on Sunday mornings. You must accept gay marriage, abortion, transgenderism, etc as a normal part of every day life and cannot refuse to participate as those practices cross your life-- bake the cake, rent out the hall, photograph the wedding, bring them into your home as roommates, provide them with abortificants, etc. And the Obama administration had sued businesses and even nuns to impose this on people of faith.

If you are a Christian and you don't know why you should oppose abortion, I suggest that you study this issue from the Bible before reading on. In modern terms, Jesus would have been an unwanted  pregnancy. They were poor, Mary was as yet unwed, they had no healthcare and they didn't have reliable transportation. God has called people from the womb to be used in His will for days they had not yet lived (cf Isaiah 49:1; Genesis 25:23; Psalm 71:6; Jeremiah 1:5, etc.). God is the one who opens and closes the womb. I am not going to make the theological and scriptural arguments here. I am simply going to assume that as a Christian this issue for you is clear and not in dispute. In fact, if your church or your pastor advocates for abortion, leave that church. You are being lied to. And when you leave, pray that they get it right. There is no genuine Christianity where abortion is advocated. I can't say it any clearer than that. It's not even an open theological debate except by disingenuous people who are promoting their agenda ungodly.

The modern way to define this issue is to obfuscate the humanity of the baby by using terms like "embryo" or "fetus."  This is not the language of the Scriptures. The term in the Bible even for infants *in utero* is baby or child. In Luke's Gospel, the baby John the Baptist in Elizabeth's womb is called βρέφος in Greek and Jesus is called the same Greek word when He is lying in the manger (Luke 1:41 & 44 cf 2:12 & 16). Don't let Satan deceive you. The humanity of preborn children is not in question. Anyone who tries to use some Scriptural basis to diminish the humanity of preborn infants is employing sophistry and deceit.

Feminism

Abortion has not only taken center stage in politics, but it has also invaded the feminist movement. This has become an article of faith in modern feminism and if you don't believe unequivocally in the unfettered killing of babies in utero, you can't be a feminist. Murdering infants is the keystone to modern feminism. Recent articles in liberal publications like The Nation have even asked "Can you be pro-life and a feminist?" with the implicit answer being "no, you can't." In the 2017 so-called "women's march," pro-life groups were specifically excluded from attending. The feminist movement has become radicalized. It is no longer about women's equality. It is simply now a subset of the identity politics being played by liberals.

So, is this merely groupthink? A herd mentality? Or, is this really an intolerance to other ideas? Today's feminism is like a purist religion that must stand or fall on all its dogmas--just as all liberalism. There is no room for heresy or discussion. Just as Al Gore said, "The science is settled. The debate is over" as it pertains to global warming, so it's also true with the infanticide and abortion death-cult called modern "feminism."

This is really a serious turn about from the roots of genuine feminism. As Christians, we ought to stand for equality of the sexes in qualitative terms. As we referred to this already, Paul made it clear that "There is neither Jew nor Greek, there is neither bond nor free, there is neither male nor female: for ye are all one in Christ Jesus" (Galatians 3:28). Second class citizenship toward women is not Christian. In Christ, we believe that men and woman may play different roles in family and society, but before God and each other we are equals.

And the hypocrisy of modern feminism couldn't be clearer. They will protest oil or gas pipelines or carbon dioxide emissions to bring the United States back to wood fire heat or even the stone age. But why won't they protest the genocide of the most vulnerable of human life? Any civil rights concerns are only addressed when it suits their liberal progressive agenda. People are simply tools to be manipulated for their votes. Many young Blacks and Hispanics are dying every day in abortion mills. But the feminists don't care. What if it were osprey eggs being destroyed? They'd be standing at the front of the line. That is why I can say that they are hypocrites...every last one of them!

Consider the way that liberal progressive views on these issues change over time. Back in the 1920's, California was considered a progressive state for forcing the eugenic sterilization of undesirables. They stood tall, proudly being on the cutting edge of a progressive agenda to engineer a great society, free of mentally deficient and other undesirable people. This was "science" serving as the new arbiter of truth. California today is still a very progressive state--perhaps the *most* progressive in the USA. It's strange how 85 years later we look back at what was considered cutting edge progressive thought and are horrified by what was done in the name of progress. I believe that many of the same things being done today will be looked back 50 years from now and people will wonder how on earth we were so barbaric. Not just abortion, but the idea of sanctuary cities, public lewdness and debauchery, and mainstreaming (or even promoting) mental illness in children through gender confusion, etc. are all on that list.

Along these lines, CBS News did a story in August 2017 about the nation of Iceland nearly eradicating Downs Syndrome. Was it some cutting edge technology that achieved this? Was it some new inoculation? Was it genetic modification to correct the gene that results in Downs? No, not at all. They aborted the unfortunate children whose amniocentesis came out positive for Downs. That's right. They killed them all.


Do black Lives *really* matter?

The issue of abortion has affected the Black community especially hard. There are some places in this country where the Black abortion rate is nearing parity with the Black birthrate. In fact, in New York City in 2012, the abortion rate for Blacks even *exceeded* that of live births. What that means in practical terms is where the KKK failed, Planned Parenthood and their ardent supporters and funders at the DNC have succeeded beyond their wildest dreams.

"Black lives matter"? That is a level of propaganda that even Joseph Goebbels would have envied. Margaret Sanger's eugenic dream of ridding society of Blacks has come true and, sadly, much of the Black clergy has helped to make it happen with the help of the Democrat Party. This must be a proud statistic for them, praise Jesus and hallelujah. Bring those pregnant Black women to Planned Parenthood and do the Lord's will. (Molech must be their lord.)

And we wonder why this country is in such moral decline? There are so-called "Christian Pastors" who stand in that pro-abortion crowd. They defend abortion as humane and some even fund abortion with ministry dollars! What do you think God sees? They must appear like what the Lord said in Isaiah 1:15 "So when you spread out your hands in prayer, I will hide My eyes from you; Yes, even though you multiply prayers, I will not listen. Your hands are covered with blood."

Thankfully there is a new generation of the Martin Luther King family in Dr. Alveda King, the niece of the civil rights icon, that has risen up and is fighting against the current atrocity that plagues not only the Black community, but every American: The denial of the right to life for the unborn. As our technology advances demonstrate more and more each day that a "fetus" is in every way just a small human being, I believe that this will likely become the next wave of the civil rights fight in America where abortions are few and rare.


## A Moral Quandry

Let me present a moral quandary for our more liberal pro-abortion friends to solve. Let's suppose that a gene is found which has very high correlation to homosexuality and is discoverable within the usual battery of tests done in an amniocentesis. Let's assume the correlation coefficient to this gene and homosexual behavior is nearly 1--meaning that it is a perfect predictor of homosexuality. Scientists announce (as they have often) that they've been able to prove that homosexuality is genetic. The gay community is excited and there is much rejoicing in their land.

Now we know that people have been using the results of amniocentesis to abort babies that have abnormalities. Back before the 2008 presidential election, liberals had suggested that Sarah Palin should have done it for her Downs son, Trig Palin, for example. But let's assume a movement forms within religious, conservative, Muslim, Jewish, Christian, Catholic groups that begins aborting babies found to have this gay gene to prevent their children from being born gay. Some of the confused Evangelicals even pronounce it as God's will. Let's say it starts catching and that nearly one million *additional* abortions a year are now being done to kill potential homosexual babies—that is on top of the over one million a year usually done. In fact, Planned Parenthood petitions their Democrat political friends to present an appropriations bill for more tax payer funding because abortions are at all time highs and the poor want to get them, too.

I would ask my liberal purist friends, would you want to see the government step in to stop that practice? Would you want a ban on all homosexual fetus abortions? Why?


Healthcare

And now that the government has put its paws in medicine and healthcare, you can be sure that socialized medicine eventually goes Frankenstein and includes abortion. You better believe it. When the government owns healthcare, by extension it owns your life, or at least controls it significantly. Mark it down. Human dignity goes out the window and dead babies become like a junkyard of auto wrecks that we can harvest parts off of. The dehumanization of life—slavery, abortion, Islamic zealotry, etc--they all have the same thing in common.

I want to say something to my fellow Black Christian brothers and sisters who are poor and struggling to make a living and I hope they take it to heart and really think this through. The liberal propaganda that has pervaded our society, our education system, our media, and even the way our recent history is being reported needs to be corrected. We are constantly being sold a bill of goods and most of us either don't care or are unaware of it. It might be because we are busy with life and don't have the time. But you at least have an obligation to your kids and grand kids.

So we need to get one thing straight here. Subtly racist white liberal Democrats look down at you and treat you paternalistically like you are some helpless ignorant child that needs their guidance and help. You are being fed crumbs from the hands of these slave masters while they have you working on their liberal progressive Democrat plantation. You've had to fight their racism and Jim Crow laws. But now your vote is being bought by promises of section 8 housing, welfare, and food stamps and these are the very things that keep you enslaved to poverty and keep you from climbing out of poverty. So I want to ask you, for some empty promises of "hope and change" and for those few crumbs you are being offered, are willing to sell yourself into slavery? Didn't you learn the lesson of the Exodus? Do you really want to go back to Egypt to eat the "cucumbers, melons, leeks, onions and garlic"?

Let me remind you that you are a child of the King! You have a place at the table, set there for *you*, and you are invited by name by the King Jesus Himself. Yet they have you supporting abortion and redefining marriage to suit their political agenda? They have you going against the Word of God? Didn't David in the Paslams say "For you created my inmost being; you knit me together in my mother's womb"? (Psalm 139:13). They couldn't even agree at their 2012 DNC convention to acknowledge God in their platform. Do you remember that fiasco? It was on TV for the whole world to see. I remind you again that my Bible says "Do not be yoked together with unbelievers. For what do righteousness and wickedness have in common? Or what fellowship can light have with darkness?" (II Corinthians 6:14). Doesn't yours?

Bottom line for me (and I hope for you, too): Before I am White, before I am a Greek, even before I am an American, before I am anything to anyone, I am a child of the King, redeemed by His blood and bought with a price. I am a Christian and I won't sell my soul for 30 pieces of silver. I won't give up my birth right for a mess of pottage. I won't be satisfied with the crumbs that are for the dogs. Please don't misunderstand me. I am not telling you to be a Republican because I am not. But you know that our Christian faith is under attack and sadly many of my Christian brothers are empowering the attackers. If that means you vote less Democrat and more Republican, so be it. And if it means you vote third party, so be it.

## Infanticide

Let me use the very sad illustration of Megan Huntsman, the Pleasant Grove, UT woman who will be spending much of the rest of her life in jail for strangling six infants she gave birth to. She was an admitted meth addict and every time she gave birth, she strangled the newborns and stored them away in bins in her garage. Truly a sad and tragic case. But how could she have avoided this tragedy? I suggest the following...

If she killed her babies the legal way, she would have simply aborted them even a few days before their birth and would have been lauded as a courageous hero by the Democrat Party. She could have been invited to give a teary-eyed speech at the Democratic National Convention praising the party's stance on unfettered and unregulated abortion up to the point of labor (parturition). She would have commended the Democrat's staunch resistance to the proposed laws compelling doctors to give aid to infants born alive during botched abortions. Pay no attention to those gasps for air and those whimpers. "Fetal tissue" has been known to do that for many years after birth. Naturally she would have received a standing ovation for her heart-warming encouragement to other women who struggle with drugs and want to terminate their baby's lives. "It would be selfish to bring a child into this world," she would say. It wasn't selfish when I spread my legs. It isn't selfish to kill the baby. It isn't selfish to deny life so I can continue to party. No. Learn to think straight.

I hate to make light of this case. But this case is simply emblematic of what is going on every day in this land of ours. We are polluting our land with the blood of innocents and God will in no wise leave us guiltless for this genocide.

Abortion and Global Warming

I have a separate chapter on the issue of Global Warming, but I want to draw a connection here to abortion. When you hear of government trying to control carbon dioxide-- which the EPA is currently doing--in order stop "global warming", few people take the time to see where this is logically heading. CO2 is what you and I exhale with every breath we take. Population control is one way to control the number of people exhaling. CO2 is also a by product of modern life--farming, transportation, heating, etc. Less people also means less CO2 emitted. If government is allowed to regulate CO2, it will be in increments, as all things are in government. First the factories, then the large buildings, then homes and cars, finally the people. They

will eventually seek to do population control--
maybe encouraging abortions (at first), or
assisting elderly and ill in "death with dignity"
campaigns, then penalizing those who have
more than 2 kids, eventually mandating a "one
child policy" (like China had). These types of
discussions are already taking place. It doesn't
take a lot of foresight to see this eventuality.

As Americans, we are often in denial about
slippery slopes and future outcomes. It is hard
for us to imagine that a government would
consider repressing people's choices to have
kids. But it has already happened in China.
And the more power we give a government,
the more they will use it. In the US, their
authority only comes from the people's
consent. Recall that the basis for our
government is just that. The phrase "consent
of the governed" is in the Declaration of
Independence. But we are at a stage where
their authority is starting to come "from the
barrel of a gun" (i.e., Mao Zedong) or from the
coercion of laws they've made to perpetuate
their own power regardless of the people. That
is Maoist Communist thinking and it is now a
regular part of American political thought. Why
do you think that as unpopular as certain
things were such as Obamacare, or wars, etc,
the opinions of the people are disregarded?
They have found ways to ignore the "consent
of the governed" and to impose their will on
us. Then they will fine, imprison or even kill
you if you don't submit.

American society is slowly going from the democracy of a representative republic, to a political class aristocracy. There are schools (Yale, Harvard, Georgetown, Princeton, etc.), there are banks/trading firms (Goldman Sachs, Morgan Stanley, Bank of America, etc.), and there are families (Kennedy, Bush, Clinton, Rockefeller, etc.) that have taken their place in this aristocracy. They make the rules. They are the *de facto* American royalty. The laws, the economy, monetary policy, federal budgets, IRS deductions and rules, etc. are all made to favor them. Welcome to the new America, where "The future's uncertain and the end is always near" (Jim Morrison and The Doors, Roadhouse Blues).

---

*Watch while I'm burned in salt*
*tell me now where's my fault*
*I'm torn in two, you pull me through*
*oh ignore my shout now scrape me out*
*Oh, nation murders me, me, me*
*suck me down your hose*
*pieces of my fingers and toes*
*use me to brew your lab rat stew*
*oh dissolve my voice for your woman's choice*
*my execution, it's your revolution*
*spill my blood on "civil" hands*
*and I pay to make you free*
*oh, nation murders me*
*yeah, with politician's dreams*
*now silencing my screams, screams, screams*
---Execution, Grammatrain

---

# Gay Marriage

Why is government involved in marriage? I ask the same question all the time. What place does the state have in giving my daughter or son permission to marry? Why do we need their permission? If I am asked whether gay marriage is acceptable, I say NO--so don't ask me. If government wasn't involved, then gays could find some gay friendly clergy and get married. I don't care. I refuse to accept that as legitimate marriage and I *ought* to have the right to refuse it without it getting shoved down my throat by a government that *demands* I accept it and even protects that opinion by the coercive force of law.

So the supreme court recently made a couple of rulings on whether gays ought to be allowed to marry. And (of course) they ruled in favor of gay marriage. I wonder why they believe they have the authority to do that? I have several friends and family members who are gay, so let me start by saying that I am not speaking from a vacuum. My faith says that their lifestyle is sin. But I will immediately tell you that I am the chiefest of sinners. That doesn't give me license to judge them, nor an excuse to keep sinning my self. All sinners need to be saved by grace, whether straight or gay. That doesn't mean God has changed His mind on gay marriages. But it does mean that we all have sin to deal with and God is in the business of restoring sinners. But government should get our of marriage.

One of the reasons this issue is getting so much play is because there have been numerous referendum votes in the states on gay marriage where the people voted against it. Then the courts have stepped in and told the people that their votes don't matter and that gays must be permitted to marry. Then the government bureaucrats in education decide to promote tolerance by teaching gay marriage and gay sex as part of their sex education curricula as early as Kindergarten. And the beat goes on.

The reason government involves itself in the marriage issue is because they control marriage. They control it for tax purposes (filing your taxes jointly or singly, for example), they control it because of property disputes (divvying up stuff in a divorce), and for many other reasons. This is why you must go to your city clerk and get a marriage license to marry. But why should they control it?

It is offensive to me, the father of four daughters, that my daughters need to get permission to marry from a bureaucrat who has no interest in their lives. I am their father and I will give their hand in marriage when I chose to, not at the whim of some bureaucrat. This entire marriage law and license system is meant to control marriage. Get the government out of it.

Since the beginning of time marriage has been a civil matter involving two families and often their clergy. I think marriage should still be that way. Let the two people who wish to marry do so in their own context. For me, that would mean they get married by a pastor in a church. For others, a priest, a rabbi, a cleric, whatever. Jump over a broom if that's your thing. I don't care and neither should the government care.

Now, if the government didn't involve itself in the gay marriage issue, then they wouldn't need to enforce a gay agenda. They wouldn't need to grant special rights to gays. If I chose to not accept gay marriage, that would be OK. I don't have to. Gay people are already living as married couples anyway. Controlling it through marital law only divides the country and often turns both sides militant.

The practical side of this would be that the schools wouldn't be compelled to teach it, the law wouldn't have to enforce it, there would be no special rights and there would be no gay agenda. Marital status should not be given any special place in housing, hiring, or education. If the owner of a duplex wants to rent the other half and he doesn't want his kids exposed to Adam and Steve's lifestyle, he should be free to decline renting to them. The Kindergarten teacher won't have to read "Heather has Two Mommies" to her 5 and 6 year olds. The Methodists won't be forced to rent out their church halls to a gay marriage ceremony.

Are there going to be gay couples getting married if the government stays out? Of course they will because they were getting married way before anyone decided to manipulate the American public for political purposes on this issue. Some churches or synagogues will marry gay couples. Most won't. Leave it alone. The government doesn't belong here. Liberals always say that they want the government out of the bedroom. Well, let's start by not controlling who they allow or disallow in it.

It makes the most amount of sense to get the government OUT of marriage and let the people decide the issue for themselves. But is that how it played out in the courts? Of course not! They simply could not help themselves from getting involved in marriage.

When the Obergefell decision came out in 2015, Chief Justice John Roberts brilliantly summed up the problem that I fear and many others of faith also fear and he did so quite eloquently! Read this artistic piece of well-reasoned logic from his dissent which I am going to quote here at length so you can understand why I am concerned:

"Federal courts are blunt instruments when it comes to creating rights. They have constitutional power only to resolve concrete cases or controversies; they do not have the flexibility of legislatures to address concerns of parties not before the court or to anticipate problems that may arise from the exercise of a new right. Today's decision,for example, creates serious questions about religious liberty. Many good and decent people oppose same-sex marriage as a tenet of faith, and their freedom to exercise religion is—unlike the right imagined by the majority—actually spelled out in the Constitution.

Respect for sincere religious conviction has led voters and legislators in every State that has adopted same-sex marriage democratically to include accommodations for religious practice. The majority's decision imposing same-sex marriage cannot, of course, create any such accommodations. The majority graciously suggests that religious believers may continue to "advocate" and "teach" their views of marriage. The First Amendment guarantees, however, the freedom to "exercise" religion. Ominously, that is not a word the majority uses.

Hard questions arise when people of faith exercise religion in ways that may be seen to conflict with the new right to same-sex marriage—when, for example, a religious college provides married student housing only to opposite-sex married couples, or a religious adoption agency declines to place children with same-sex married couples. Indeed, the Solicitor General candidly acknowledged that the tax exemptions of some religious institutions would be in question if they opposed same-sex marriage. There is little doubt that these and similar questions will soon be before this Court. Unfortunately, people of faith can take no comfort in the treatment they receive from the majority today.

Perhaps the most discouraging aspect of today's decision is the extent to which the majority feels compelled to sully those on the other side of the debate. The majority offers a cursory assurance that it does not intend to disparage people who, as a matter of conscience, cannot accept same-sex marriage. That disclaimer is hard to square with the very next sentence, in which the majority explains that "the necessary consequence" of laws codifying the traditional definition of marriage is to "demean or stigmatize" same-sex couples. The majority reiterates such characterizations over and over. By the majority's account, Americans who did nothing more than follow the understanding of marriage that has existed for our entire history —in particular, the tens of millions of people who voted to reaffirm their States' enduring definition of marriage—have acted to "lock...out," "disparage," "disrespect and subordinate," and inflict "dignitary wounds" upon their gay and lesbian neighbors. These apparent assaults on the character of fair minded people will have an effect, in society and in court. Moreover, they are entirely gratuitous. It is one thing for the majority to conclude that the Constitution protects a right to same-sex marriage; it is something else to portray everyone who does not share the majority's "better informed understanding" as bigoted." (Obergefell, Roberts Dissent)

So was Justice Roberts right? In February 2017 Washington State Supreme Court affirmed lower court ruling concerning a 71 year old Christian florist, Mrs. Barronelle Stutzman, who refused to create wedding floral arrangements for a gay couple on the basis of the Biblical prohibitions against gay marriage. She was heavily fined because in Washington State your First Amendment religious rights of conscience cannot excuse you from participating in the planning and execution of a gay wedding. The state court ruled that the First Amendment clause which forbids the government from "prohibiting the free exercise" of religion is an invalid defense. Instead of going to another florist, the gay couple wanted to sue her to make their point and they won.

The Washington State constitution expressly states that citizens have "freedom of conscience in all matters of religious sentiment," but religious sentiments on gay marriage apparently are not protected. In fact, the ruling states explicitly that she "must provide full wedding support for same-sex ceremonies, including custom design work to decorate the ceremony, delivery to the forum, staying at the ceremony to touch up arrangements, and assisting the wedding party." In other words, her full participation and attendance at the wedding is required by this ruling. Is that fair?

The state tried to settle with her to avoid continuing this embarrassment. In effect, they said to her they will let her get away with a mere $2001 in fines and fees as long as she agrees to deny her faith and do what they tell her from now on. Of course, she refused the offer. The Washington State attorney general couldn't understand why she wouldn't take the offer. This type of thinking basically implies that the First Amendment doesn't apply to living out your faith by your deeds, only to what is in your brain.

"Our state would be a better place if we respected each others differences, and our leaders protected the freedom to have those differences," wrote Mrs. Stutzman. "Because I follow the Bible's teaching that marriage is the union of one man and one woman, I am no longer free to act on my beliefs."

What I believe we are seeing is a constitutional interpretation which relegates "the free exercise thereof" of religion to the four walls of a church. It says, basically, that you are only permitted to live out your faith on Sunday mornings at 11 a.m., but you must check that faith at the door when you are leaving the building because in the world you cannot practice what your faith teaches.

The First Amendment states that "Congress shall make no law respecting an establishment of religion, or prohibiting the free exercise thereof..." But the current interpretation of that amendment seems to do several things.

1) Respect the disestablishment of religion
2) Prohibits its free exercise
3) Relegates this protection only to churches and clergy (so far)

But, as a constitutional right, it is supposed to be for all the citizens. Yet it no longer seems to be so but now is only for clergy.

These unintended consequences (or, perhaps they *are* intended) demonstrate why the government should stay out of the marriage issue all together. I have said this many times and I am saying it again right here. I don't care what two adults do in regards to marriage, or sex, or anything else and I don't want to care and I shouldn't have to care.

I don't care that SCOTUS voted to allow gay marriage in all 50 states as much as I care that this will be used to discriminate against those who don't want anything to do with gay marriage. What I do care about is whether they will now sue 80 year old Aunt Bea because she refuses to play the organ for their wedding? And if she has a stroke that night from the duress and stress of the ordeal, will they accept responsibility? Will they take Miss Tilly's home because she doesn't want to bake a cake or create flower arrangements for it (like they did Mrs. Barronelle Stutzman, the florist in Washington State)? Will Rev. Smith have to preform the wedding because he is licensed by the state? What about Rabbi Goldberg? What about Imam Ahmed? Will the state revoke their license if they refuse? Will Menachem Levin (a devout Orthodox Jew) be forced to photograph the wedding or lose everything? Will Christ Holiness Church be forced to accommodate the wedding in their chapel because they have tax exempt status?

Don't give me your rationale today. Answer this five or ten years from now when the inevitable unintended consequences will abound. Mark my words. They already have.

The irony of some of the rulings after the Obergefell decision is found within the decision itself...

"Finally, it must be emphasized that religions, and those who adhere to religious doctrines, may continue to advocate with utmost, sincere conviction that, by divine precepts, same-sex marriage should not be condoned. The First Amendment ensures that religious organizations and persons are given proper protection as they seek to teach the principles that are so fulfilling and so central to their lives and faiths, and to their own deep aspirations to continue the family structure they have long revered." (Obergefell v. Hodges)

Though Justice Kennedy added those words to his ruling in Obergefell, the truth is that people who hold to marriage as sacred as taught in the Bible have been sued and have been forced to submit to demands by gay litigants or pay heavy fines, lose their businesses, and go out of business.

Government is *not* the answer to our duties to the Gospel of Jesus Christ. Getting people saved by believing in the blood sacrifice of Jesus on the cross is! Consider the two-party political system's approach to gay marriage. One side wants to legalize gay marriage, which makes my side want to put up a marriage amendment, which will then end up being thrown out in the supreme court one day, etc. etc. We thought Clinton's D.O.M.A. (Defense of Marriage Act) and his "Don't Ask, Don't Tell" policy would be the end of it. But it wasn't. We've allowed politics to bamboozle us again.

So I say that we get the government out of the marriage issue all together! Let the government not regulate marriage at all. It offends me that my daughter needs to go to the court house to get a license to marry. After all, I am her father. I ought to be the one who gives her hand in marriage--not some judge or civil clerk! When the government involves itself in that issue, we end up with what we have today. And, knowing the history of US jurisprudence, "gay rights" will end up being forced on us because they are giving gays the same minority status like they did for Blacks, Hispanics, women, religious minorities, etc. That ought to be an offense to anyone who believes (like I do) in Martin Luther King's philosophy of civil rights.

As a believer, I suspect other believers would prefer a totally secular, minimal government that will not interfere with the affairs of people over a government that wades into the waters of issues which offend us. I prefer a government that takes no stance on homosexual marriage (for example) than one which affirms it and then gives them special civil rights. What's next, affirmative action for gays? You understand my point. Government should get out of the issue of marriage and leave that issue up to pastors or rabbis or whatever clergy there is. That way, I will be free to accept or reject a "couple" without the law telling me I must accept them under the coercive penalty of law.

Sinners will sin. That is no surprise. But don't let the government tell me I must accept their sin as normative and try to teach my kids about it in school as an alternative lifestyle.


The Christian Case

I have to conclude this chapter by making the Christian case against gay marriage. When Jesus was approached about the issue of divorce, his answer to the Pharisees also gave us His view of marriage. The passage is Matthew 19:3-6,

"Some Pharisees came to Jesus, testing Him and asking, "Is it lawful for a man to divorce his wife for any reason at all?" And He answered and said, "Have you not read that He who created them from the beginning MADE THEM MALE AND FEMALE, and said, 'FOR THIS REASON A MAN SHALL LEAVE HIS FATHER AND MOTHER AND BE JOINED TO HIS WIFE, AND THE TWO SHALL BECOME ONE FLESH'? "So they are no longer two, but one flesh. What therefore God has joined together, let no man separate."

Now consider that Jesus' argument against divorce also applies to gay marriage. He defined marriage as the union of male and female as one flesh and that no man should separate them. He specifically pointed to the two genders as that which joins together as one.

What Jesus was quoting was obviously from Genesis 2:34 where the words appear verbatim, "For this reason a man shall leave his father and his mother, and be joined to his wife; and they shall become one flesh."

Though He didn't go into it in further detail, surely Jesus saw the way male and female were created as the basis for marriage. In that Genesis passage, there is a specific order to how that unfolded. The passage in Genesis 2:18-23 reads,

Then the LORD God said, "It is not good for the man to be alone; I will make him a helper suitable for him." Out of the ground the LORD God formed every beast of the field and every bird of the sky, and brought them to the man to see what he would call them; and whatever the man called a living creature, that was its name. The man gave names to all the cattle, and to the birds of the sky, and to every beast of the field, but for Adam there was not found a helper suitable for him. So the LORD God caused a deep sleep to fall upon the man, and he slept; then He took one of his ribs and closed up the flesh at that place. The LORD God fashioned into a woman the rib which He had taken from the man, and brought her to the man. The man said, "This is now bone of my bones, And flesh of my flesh; she shall be called Woman, because she was taken out of Man."

We see here several things. First, after God was finished creating the heavens and the earth, He created man—Adam—alone. God had pronounced after each successive act of creation "And God saw that it was good." Six times in the first chapter of Genesis He said that and after His works were completed, it says in Genesis 1:31 that "God saw all that He had made, and behold, it was very good."

But all was not perfect in God's creation. After making those pronouncements about the goodness of His works, it says in Genesis 2:18 "Then the LORD God said, It is not good for the man to be alone; I will make him a helper suitable for him." This would be the first time that God pronounced something to be "not good" in His brand new creation. This is not by accident. God wanted to teach us a lesson here and that lesson started with Adam. He was going to answer a fundamental question in this creative act.

The issue that God pointed out was that it was "not good" that man was alone. God then proceeded to parade all the animals before Adam and Adam took to naming them. It would almost seem as if this was a non sequitur. But God wanted to teach Adam an object lesson that went something like this: Yes, dog might be a man's best friend and keeping a cat might be good for a pet. A man and his horse might make for a great western movie. The animals that I made may all be pretty cool. But here is what I want you to see, "...but for Adam there was not found a helper suitable for him" (Genesis 2:20).

What God then did was to put Adam to sleep and form a woman out of a piece of Adam's side. When he woke up he immediately knew what this was about. Here is the lesson: God's answer for man's loneliness is a woman. It wasn't a man. In fact, when a man chooses another man for his mate, he is rejecting God's answer. Remember that God specifically said in Genesis 2:18 "I will make him a helper suitable for him." Eve was that "suitable helper." This is specifically the expressed created reason that heterosexual marriage is the plan of God. It is only because of sin that mankind meddled with this most fundamental truth. Male and female must come together to fulfill God's purpose in creation. Adam's reaction to Eve was exactly what God intended. He receives her and they become one flesh. She was literally the woman of his dreams.

Christians don't hate gay people. But marriage is not what God intended for gay people. This is a fundamental point from the Bible and the Supreme Court deciding that gay marriage is allowable doesn't validate it. It only makes the United States hostile to the Word of God.

# Transgenderism

It was spring of 2016 during the last year of president Obama's administration that the decision was made to be on the cutting edge of the deviancy issues. And I wish to offer thanks to everyone who voted him in--twice! I say that with obvious sarcasm. Never did a single administration do so much to change marriage, sexuality, sexual identity, and anything sexual than did Barack Obama. His fixation on issues pertaining to sex will forever have an effect on this nation. That is not an overstatement.

Lest you misunderstand what my point is, I want to make it clear here. You and I cannot change what people do in their bedrooms. We cannot pass effective laws against homosexuality or cross dressing or transgenderism. We can't change what people's sexual kinks are, nor can we control their behaviors. These are issues of the heart and, as Christians, we ought to be focused on spreading the message of Jesus' love and redemption to sinners—including those who have sexual deviancy issues. That alone will resolve this because the New Testament teaches us that it is by grace, not by law, that Christians are supposed to operate. We sing "Amazing grace how sweet the sound that saved a wretch like me." I hope that we also believe that it is by grace that this (and all sin) can be dealt with effectively.

Yet, in his final year in office, the Obama administration issued a sweeping directive telling every public school district in the country to allow transgender students to use the bathrooms that match their gender identity. This directive was felt all the way down to the local level—including my hometown in Southern New Jersey. A letter to school districts went out making the declaration and signed by both Justice and Education department officials that described what schools should do to ensure that none of their students are discriminated against.

This directive did not have the force of law, but it contained an implicit threat that any schools that did not abide by the Obama administration's interpretation of the law could face lawsuits or a loss of federal aid. This had an effect on local school systems (as it did my own) that still hasn't been resolved.

I want to pause here for a moment and say that there is never a place in the message of Jesus for hate toward our fellow man. We can hate what is being done—especially if it is subversive to our families or our faith. But we cannot hate people. This includes both the political class that attempts to impose this folly upon us, nor the ones toward which this folly is targeted. I feel sorry for those who have gender confusion issues.

Lavern Cox is a famous actress/actor of the "shemale" variety. In April of 2015 Cox decide to pose in the nude for Allure Magazine. At the time, the world celebrated the nude poses of this transsexual shemale. "Look!" they said, "He/she is so passable as a woman!" People like this put this type of deviancy in the public spotlight. I am not using the word deviancy as a pejorative. I am using it in its definitional sense: This behavior deviates from the biological and social norms.

When I read about this person, it was not because I was interested in gawking. I read about him/her because I wondered with great sorrow what drives a person to this behavior and to such extremes? In a society so fixated on appearances and sex, that type of spectacle seems to be the epitome. This is where it has come to. It's sad how we objectify people like this. It's sad how far people will go to get attention. What would Lavern Cox have done if he/she lived one hundred years ago? Or, if he/she was born in Zimbabwe? We call this freedom. We call this total liberation. But I say this is a deep psychological and spiritual problem. I feel bad for Cox. The media and the general population sees him/her as a freak show. And perhaps she/he might relish in that role. And I am sure that someone will read this and I will be attacked for being heartless when it is really I who has a heart for him/her. Laverne, I can only pray that one day you find yourself and your purpose in life. I say this for you and the many others out there who are searching for answers to their gender, sexual and role confusion.

And I think (lest some get me wrong) I should state clearly that I am not judging this person for the struggle they are having. I am judging society for objectifying this person and turning him/her into a freak show. And I am not convinced that gender reassignment is the right approach for someone who has these struggles. I've never walked in their shoes so I can only pray that one day they find their self and purpose in life. She/he may feel they have. Or, maybe 10 years down the road he/she may feel different about this.

I will be the first to admit that there is a wide spectrum of maleness and femaleness in people's DNA presentation. Some girls are very feminine and some girls are more masculine. Some boys are very masculine and some are more effeminate. How they deal with that is the issue. It is clear that it is society that drives this behavior. As evidence, I will again suggest that this was extremely rare even here in the USA a century ago. I believe that in many instances these people end up having serious social and emotional problems years down the road. Maybe that is also society's fault. But maybe not.

Unfortunately, suicide is another psychological problem that seems to have a higher incidence with people going through identity crisis. And transgenderism is certainly an identity crisis. That is why there is more to this issue than simply this one example.

Psychologist Eric Erickson places the point of gender identity (i.e., Identity vs Role Confusion) in children's development at 12-18 years old. That is middle school into high school. Thankfully, most people who think about suicide never do it. But that doesn't mean that their situation isn't as tough (or even tougher) than those who do and succeed. Some people experience mental states that leave them weak, self-centered, and short-sighted. Those people are the ones who also attempt suicide and too often succeed. I've had the sad experience of counseling with three such people. All three had various presentations of schizophrenia and all three took their own lives.

These people are subject to too many agendas. A transgendered person is looking for a purpose in his/her life and a segment of society has exploited him/her as a freak show. How do we know this? Because Lavern Cox has become a news story. Just like every shooting of a Black person is exploited by Al Sharpton as a poster-child for his agenda, this person is being exploited (through celebration) as poster-child for an agenda. And the politicians have grabbed on to this and taken it for a ride.

Biblically, we live in a fallen creation, not a pristine one. Every day people are born with defects, people get sicknesses, people die. That is not the way it was designed. You can read what the Apostle Paul wrote to the Romans 8:18ff on this point. Some people with hateful agendas love to project their own hate on Christians and say that Christians are simply haters, and that we secretly hate gay people. But the truth is that we see what the Scriptures teach and want to love the person enough to show him the answer to their struggles. We want to share the joy that we ourselves have found.

And let me address the word "freak," because I said that society sees this person as a freak and some may take offense to this term. Most people won't admit it, but it's like seeing a bearded woman, or a dwarf, or even a man without limbs. They treat them as objects for the satisfaction of their curiosity. It's why people stop and stare when there is a bad car accident. It's why some people love to see gore. I feel bad for these people because they are being objectified. It isn't right that society do this. But, in the case of Lavern Cox, he/she is even finding purpose in his/her own objectification which, to me, makes it doubly sad. If what he/she is doing will help someone not kill himself, then I guess that it an upside. I am not sure that is true.

Then there is the case Debi Jackson, the

mother of a child who was born as a boy but began allowing her son to identify as a girl. There is no way in describing this other than to say that this mother is perpetrating a form of Munchausen syndrome by proxy on her kid. Except, instead of slowly killing her kid by poisoning his food (as most cases), she is poisoning his mind and his soul. She seeks attention by being the mother of the youngest transgender kid ever and apparently she's willing to sacrifice her kid for the attention. She may even have an activist agenda at this point because she finds her sense of community within that group. And we live in such a politically correct world that no one dare speak out against it. In fact, there are some medical professionals (e.g., psychologists, etc.) who are searching for the most bizarre cases and they are intellectually validating them by adding the gravitas of their "training" and degree, which has now become a new path to celebrity for them.

All of what I wrote concerning Lavern Cox also applies here. But this case has the added dimension of being perpetrated upon a young child. This is not normal and Ms. Jackson ought to be investigated for child abuse.

To end this section on transgenderism, I would like to quote extensively from the American Academy of Pediatrics about the issue:

*Gender Ideology Harms Children*
*(Updated May 2017)*

*The American College of Pediatricians urges healthcare professionals, educators and legislators to reject all policies that condition children to accept as normal a life of chemical and surgical impersonation of the opposite sex. Facts – not ideology – determine reality.*

*1. Human sexuality is an objective biological binary trait: "XY" and "XX" are genetic markers of male and female, respectively – not genetic markers of a disorder. The norm for human design is to be conceived either male or female. Human sexuality is binary by design with the obvious purpose being the reproduction and flourishing of our species. This principle is self-evident. The exceedingly rare disorders of sex development (DSDs), including but not limited to testicular feminization and congenital adrenal hyperplasia, are all medically identifiable deviations from the sexual binary norm, and are rightly recognized as disorders of human design. Individuals with DSDs (also referred to as "intersex") do not constitute a third sex.1*

*2. No one is born with a gender. Everyone is born with a biological sex. Gender (an awareness and sense of oneself as male or female) is a sociological and psychological concept; not an objective biological one. No one is born with an awareness of themselves* as male or female; this awareness develops over time and, like all developmental processes, may be derailed by a child's subjective perceptions, relationships, and adverse experiences from infancy forward. People who identify as "feeling like the opposite sex" or "somewhere in between" do not comprise a third sex. They remain biological men or biological women.2,3,4

3. A person's belief that he or she is something they are not is, at best, a sign of confused thinking. When an otherwise healthy biological boy believes he is a girl, or an otherwise healthy biological girl believes she is a boy, an objective psychological problem exists that lies in the mind not the body, and it should be treated as such. These children suffer from gender dysphoria. Gender dysphoria (GD), formerly listed as Gender Identity Disorder (GID), is a recognized mental disorder in the most recent edition of the Diagnostic and Statistical Manual of the American Psychiatric Association (DSM-V).5 The psychodynamic and social learning theories of GD/GID have never been disproved.2,4,5

4. Puberty is not a disease and puberty-blocking hormones can be dangerous. Reversible or not, puberty- blocking hormones induce a state of disease – the absence of puberty – and inhibit growth and fertility in a previously biologically healthy child.6

*5. According to the DSM-V, as many as 98% of gender confused boys and 88% of gender confused girls eventually accept their biological sex after naturally passing through puberty.5*

*6. Pre-pubertal children diagnosed with gender dysphoria may be given puberty blockers as young as eleven, and will require cross-sex hormones in later adolescence to continue impersonating the opposite sex. These children will never be able to conceive any genetically related children even via articifial reproductive technology. In addition, cross-sex hormones (testosterone and estrogen) are associated with dangerous health risks including but not limited to cardiac disease, high blood pressure, blood clots, stroke, diabetes, and cancer.7,8,9,10,11*

*7. Rates of suicide are nearly twenty times greater among adults who use cross-sex hormones and undergo sex reassignment surgery, even in Sweden which is among the most LGBTQ – affirming countries.12 What compassionate and reasonable person would condemn young children to this fate knowing that after puberty as many as 88% of girls and 98% of boys will eventually accept reality and achieve a state of mental and physical health?*

*8. Conditioning children into believing a lifetime of chemical and surgical impersonation of the opposite sex is normal and healthful is child abuse. Endorsing gender discordance as normal via public education and legal policies will confuse children and parents, leading more children to present to "gender clinics" where they will be given puberty-blocking drugs. This, in turn, virtually ensures they will "choose" a lifetime of carcinogenic and otherwise toxic cross-sex hormones, and likely consider unnecessary surgical mutilation of their healthy body parts as young adults.*

To be sure, the Christian perspective on this issue is in agreement with the science. Gender is something that starts from the time you are conceived. It determines your formation in the womb, the way you will mature, the way you think and much of the remainder of your life on earth. The binary physiology of males and female is also the way we were created to procreate and perpetuate ourselves. Adding gender confusion to that mix only serves to frustrate and derail what is biologically natural. And humans now have the ability to overcome their biology by their free willed choices. A man can become a woman and a woman can become a man by hormone therapy and surgery. But that doesn't make it so.

# War on Poverty

The problem with modern American poverty is that it has not been resolved by government action and, in fact, a strong case can be made that government action has actually made it worse in many ways.

The way we treat the poor and vulnerable in our society says a lot about who we are. The federal government has given the American people an excuse to not personally care about the poor. Instead of "loving our neighbor as ourselves" like Jesus taught, we now outsource compassion to the faceless bureaucracy. This way, when we see a poor person begging for money on the street we can just walk by and think "Why doesn't he get some benefits?" The parable of the Good Samaritan teaches that it is you, not someone else's job to help the suffering. When you outsource compassion for the poor to a bureaucracy, you get Kitty Genovese syndrome among the population. You may recall, nobody helped her because everyone thought someone else would. Or, that it was not their business. She ended up getting raped and stabbed multiple times and died.

There have been several anti-poverty measures that the federal government had in place since the Great Depression. But ever since the federal government got heavily involved in the poverty business back in 1960's under Lyndon B. Johnson's "war on poverty" they have funded that war on poverty with social security money (which is now under funded), spent multiple trillions of dollars on it, and the poverty rates have remained basically the same. So, in effect, what these programs did was *not* to end poverty, but to fund poverty as a life choice and way of life. We perpetuated it.

The great difference between Roosevelt and Johnson is that the poverty programs that started under Franklin D. Roosevelt had sunset provisions in them to prevent poverty becoming a matter of a lifestyle choice. As much as I disagreed with many of his policies, there was wisdom in that idea. He also didn't simply hand out money, but had criteria that needed to be met and dovetailed the help with other programs such as surplus food going to feeding programs.

But Johnson's policies had no such wisdom and he used primarily the working class Social Security money to fund his "war on poverty." The result is generations of people who have made poverty a lifestyle choice. Getting your benefits has become a rite of passage in some communities I have worked with. That's not to say it is not needed at all. But we have not used discernment or wisdom in handing out these benefits. There seems to be little accountability. And many have used this as a racial issue to sow discord and manipulate that for political gain. This shouldn't be.

Civil unrest is one thing that I believe becomes an inevitable outcome of people who become overly dependent on the government for their life and well-being. It will only get worse as more and more people become dependent and their ability to care for their own needs decreases. When you fund poverty, you only get more poverty. When you incentivize dependence, you get more dependence. In my opinion, the failures we've seen this past decade in the poor neighborhoods in cities like Ferguson, New York City and Baltimore tell a bigger story about our society. I believe we've gutted the poor family through our government interventions.

Government dependence leads to a dead-end life. You have nothing to look forward to but a check, a refilled EBT card, the same housing, the same TV programming, the same "hood." Your life becomes no different than that of a caged animal and your humanity is traded for the security of your "basic" needs on Maslow's pyramid. You never reach anything near self-actualization. Government involvement in poverty has decimated the family unit and has created generations of people utterly unable to help themselves. By funding poverty as a lifestyle we have discouraged marriage because welfare benefits typically cease when you marry. We've housed the poor in projects and have given them section 8 vouchers to make ourselves feel good and decieve ourselves into believing we have help alleviate poverty. We have told the poor to get educated, but have lowered the standards of education to the point that a high school diploma--especially one from an urban area--is almost worthless.

When people don't have to struggle to survive, when they have no productive career or business endeavors to pour themselves into, they often fall into living the futility of a meaningless and mundane life. It is unfortunately part of human nature. You see the eccentric children of the wealthy getting into all sorts of deviant behaviors and pursuits which are only kept in check by the company they keep. But in the poor neighborhoods, the same basic principal is in play. People who have all their basic needs met by the government have no struggle to meet their own basic needs. They are housed, fed, clothed etc. with very little effort, giving them a life full of free time. So there is plenty of time for watching TV, fighting in the streets, drugs and sex, etc. It's not all the poor, but enough of them that the neighborhood descends into chaos. Consider that if they worked, that alone would be 8-10 hours less time available for futile pursuits. This is why, in what seems to be a dead-end life, the "Gangsta Hip Hop" lifestyle looks like a way to success. Selling drugs looks like a way to success. "Pimping ho's" looks like a way to success. The results are obvious when the drug dealer in your own neighborhood drives a

Benz, or the well-dressed pimp is surrounded by his pretty women. In the words of Sigmund Freud "Lieben und Arbeiten" (i.e., to love and to work) is what's missing.

The effect is a cumulative systemic abuse of the poor by the political class who want to keep them dependent. But there is also a cumulative systemic abuse inflicted on the working and middle class of America at the hands of poverty zealots who masquerade as politicians caring for the poor. These politicians use theoretical academic constructs of poverty rather than real life poor. They are abstractions of those grasping for straws against the obvious.

It will take radical change to stop and reverse this process. It isn't really a racial issue. But it has especially and disproportionately affected the Black family. Special interests, liberals, government unions, and especially Democrats, will all have to relinquish their hold and stop the propaganda and divisiveness if this problem is going to be solved. Deep down they know that liberalism has been an utter failure and disservice to these constituents. Nearly every American city shows this to be true and they are almost all run by Democrats—in many cases for decades. But manipulating the poor has been their path to political power. And their twisted "morality" actually makes them believe that they are doing right. They need to wake up and really see their own results. The burning, decaying, blighted, crime and drug-ridden neighborhoods overwhelmingly vote for these people because they've been told that they are the only ones who care and that Republicans or Conservatives don't care if you are dead.

I already know that liberals will attack what I am saying. The tragedy of modern liberalism is that it often lends itself to mindless assent, groupthink and herd mentality. It buys the goods without discernment and critique because it often deals in emotion rather fact. And, even when facts are posited, they are usually massaged to fit the narrative, rather than assessed to lead one to the truth. And when someone offers an alternative view, they are treated like Galilio before the keepers defending that Ptolemaic solar system. Confirmation bias is difficult to see when it is *you* who is experiencing it.

Finally, in my church duties I have worked with the poor for over thirty years. I have helped poor and struggling people firsthand. Not in theory, not for photo-ops like the politicians do, but in fact--real life people. When someone criticizes you for taking a conservative or libertarian view on these issues, it is appropriate to ask them "Have you worked a homeless shelter? Have you dealt with section 8 housing recipients, or Temporary Rental Assistance recipients? Food stamps, EBT, SNAP, welfare, Food Bank, etc?" Some politician taking money from your pocket to fund a poverty program isn't helping the poor. It's opportunism that has cost him nothing. In fact, he's stolen your glory because it was your money he gave out! Those immersed in maintaining a public facade by their narcissistic introspections cannot see the pain and suffering of those people they walk past because the mirror before them blocks their view. That is our politicians.

The truth is that Christians regularly help people and many do so out of their own pocket. Most help ministries for the poor and homeless were established by Christians and funded by them. I am quite honestly sick and tired of the abstractions liberals pose when they speak of this issue. They "care" for some "abstract poor" whom they have never met but envision in their warped brains as destitute and hungry. They want to help him with other people's money, through proxies and by government largess. It's ridiculous.
I take *no one* seriously who says they care about the poor but have never actually gone to their homes, fed them, helped them with their own money, had them over for dinner, etc. It's a ruse, folks. It's just hot air and amounts to nothing.  As Jesus' own brother James wrote in James 2:14-17,

"What use is it, my brethren, if someone says he has faith but he has no works? Can that faith save him? If a brother or sister is without clothing and in need of daily food, and one of you says to them, "Go in peace, be warmed and be filled," and yet you do not give them what is necessary for their body, what use is that? Even so faith, if it has no works, is dead, being by itself."

The government by its war on poverty has created more poverty because it has emasculated what is the traditional role of men as providers and has told women you don't need a man. You don't need a provider. You don't need a protector. Your Uncle Sam's got a whole load of money that he steals from working people and he'll help you raise your kids. He will feed you, clothe you, get you medical care and housing and energy costs-- even a phone. You don't need a man because Uncle Sam *is* your man. And even if you decide afterward to kill one of your unborn kids (abortion), its OK because Uncle Sam will make sure there is a neighborhood baby killer right there to help you out with that. Uncle Sam will pay his rent and utilities and worker's salaries to make sure the killer has a place to perform his child sacrifices in one of those rooms--a place in your neighborhood--all under the cover of law. We shall call it "women's healthcare."

Doesn't this cause poverty? No, the government is only there to help. They say follow the money. But never follow the money if it leads you to poverty. And what about crime? No, It can't Uncle Sam's fault. Women being objectified? No, that's right wing talk. We got us a nice little plantation for all of you poor folks--White, Black, Hispanic, Oriental...your Uncle Sam doesn't discriminate. Welcome to the ghetto.

83

# War on Drugs

I recently read that Afghanistan is producing record amounts of Opium and the USA is undergoing a heroin epidemic. Isn't that awesome?! Cool beans! The charity "Wounded Warrior Project" has pictures of the injuries our soldiers sustained to help make this happen! (They do NOT exploit their injuries for donations. Nevertheless, there are numerous photos of them there.) Our troops fought bravely and put their lives and limbs on the line literally so that our politicians can squander their sacrifice by allowing (among other things) the bolstering of their opium production. All this is of course because the "war on drugs" is big business in the US. The trial lawyers association are mega big time contributors to the DNC and enjoy the vast opportunities that can be exploited in its prosecution. And let's not forget the jails, law enforcement, drug rehabs, the judiciary, etc.

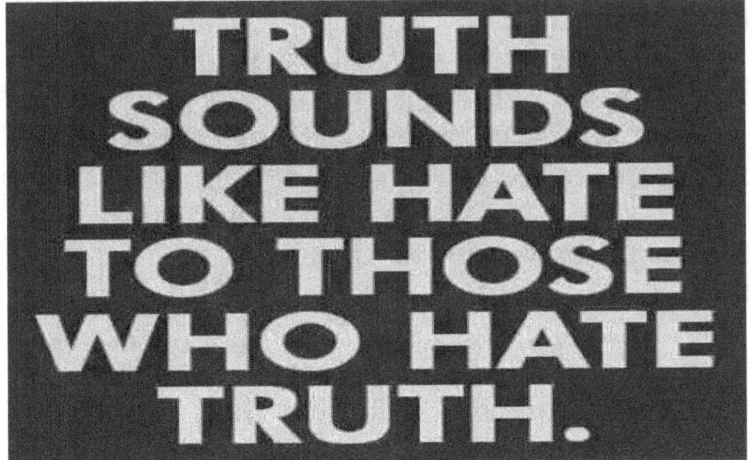

SO, let's look at the bright side of this: This rise in opium production will be a boon to the US economy! At least some are "happy, happy, happy" to see this! (Speaking the truth sometimes bothers some people...I'm sorry. Obviously I am being sarcastic here.)

The issue of drugs is a very personal one to me. I had a nephew whom we called Stevie that died of a drug overdose. He left behind two beautiful daughters and an unborn son. Those girls will never have their daddy tuck them in at night. Another man will raise those kids. His mother and father will never be completely whole again.  How can they be? There is an empty place at the table every time they have a family gathering. There is currently a heroin epidemic going on in the US and something needs to be done. I want to propose something different.

I admit at the outset that this is one of the more controversial aspects of my Christian libertarianism. But I am simply asking that you think about what I am writing here. That we have a drug problem in this country is obvious. How to solve it is a different matter. Many people advocate the current system of a strong eradication approach using harsher law, stricter enforcement, more searches, more interdiction, more law enforcement techniques, dogs, x-rays, cameras, etc. They tell us that it will never be perfect, but that these measures are increasingly stemming the flow of drugs into the country. I must ask how true that is, is it working, and at what cost?

The illegal drug traffic into the USA is not slowing down. By every measure available, more drugs flow into the USA every year and illegal drug use has remained the same over the years. Often, the drugs being abused have just changed from one type to another. Currently, the biggie is heroin and it's killing many people! Yet, we spend more money every year on combating this problem. So I suggest that maybe it's time we tried another approach.

This is really a lesson of basic economics. I want to repeat what I wrote at the outset of this book. The Bible tells us in I Timothy 6:10 that "The love of money is the root of ALL evil" and the drug war is the evidence to prove it. What makes the drug trade so lucrative is the fact that they are illegal. That means that they will command a premium price because of the efforts it takes to deliver them. But what that also means is that the delivery process is treacherous. People are getting killed every day and violence is a very real part of this underground economy. In fact, most of the violence we see in society comes from illegal drugs. Let me repeat that: MOST of the violence we see in our society comes from illegal drugs. Innocent people, guilty people, law enforcement, and little kids all get caught in the crossfire of the drug trade. All of this is the *direct* result of drugs being illegal. There's lots of money to be made and people will kill for it. Nobody will kill or be willing to risk being killed for sand, rocks, or sea shells. But drugs can be very lucrative.

There are nearly 2,000,000 people in jails and prisons across the USA for various drug crimes. When you add in the associated crimes—the murders, gang activity, violence, thefts, etc,--it becomes nearly three quarters of the people in jail are there for some drug related offense. The money we spend on police, courts, lawyers, judges, jails, interdiction efforts on the high seas and along the borders is enormous! But the price we pay in society for dead kids, grieving mothers, childless fathers, fatherless children, and broken lives can't be counted.

By continuing the drug was as it stands the government has created a monster! I guess that the days of Prohibition didn't teach us a lesson. Those who fail to learn from history are doomed to repeat it and we certainly are repeating it. It was Prohibition that gave us Al Capone and the St. Valentine's Day massacre. It was during Prohibition that we saw violence in families and in society rise, not fall. Yet, we are taking the same approach today. We are creating violence because of drugs being illegal. I've never seen anyone shot and killed for booze "territory," but it USED to happen during Prohibition with Al Capone and those types. The same thing is happening now with drugs. People are killing each other and innocent by-standers over street-corners that they see as "their territory."

Let me add another important point: Most of the money from drugs goes to support crime and terrorism. That is a fact. If drugs were made legal, that money would mostly stay in the USA and NONE would go to support crime and terrorism. The amount of money is tremendous. Worldwide, we are talking nearly about close to a half trillion dollars. That's money going into Columbia, Mexico, Afghanistan and El Salvadore. We are funding people who routinely behead and shoot their opponents. Drug money is funding those who fund terrorism.

When you read this approach it is easy to accuse me of wanting to legalize drugs because I have an interest in using them, or some other such conflict. But I am not advocating drug use, nor do I think that making them legal is good for society. I am only saying that making them legal is *better* than what we are doing now. If you ever saw the orphaned kids, the grief and misery of a mother crying and wailing because her son was shot dead by a drug dealer, or her little girl was shot while playing hopscotch nearby on the sidewalk, you may reevaluate it. We are making drugs very profitable for the dealers and pushers by keeping them illegal. Cops are getting killed, drug addicts are dying, first time users are dying, numerous innocents are dying and dealers are dying--all because of the profit motive. If we take away the profits, this new vintage of "Al Capones" won't make money any more.

Could it be that the special interests actually *want* a constant war? Maybe the police unions, courts, jails, and various government agencies fear that legalization will cost them their jobs. And they are probably right. But the billions that we now spend on this violent war will be used to build a better society instead of sustaining a violent one. It makes more sense that we treat drug use as a health issue which will be much cheaper and doesn't need violence.

Think about it: Under the current system, the only ones profiting are the dealers, kingpins, drug lords and everyone who is in the legal system. The current drug war is providing lots of money to both sides of the equation—the criminals and the law-- and it is all coming out of your wallet and mine. If we take away their profits by regulating drugs the same way that we do alcohol and by making them legal but controlled, and this whole violent underground economy crumbles. If we made drugs legal, taxed and regulated them like cigarettes or beer, it would take away the profit motive in the cities. No more dealers, pushers, thugs, gangstas, etc. No more drive-by shootings, turf wars, violence, etc. They would be regulated like beer and the money we save as a society would *easily* be enough to help the people who get hooked. The rest of the money could go toward better streets, bridges, schools and parks. And there is an added benefit to this. There will no longer be the chance that some addict gets a batch of impure stuff that causes an overdose death. No drugs cut with Ajax or rat poison. There would be quality control just like with any other consumable product.

Some will say that this will increase the drug problem. But the countries that have tried this haven't seen any increases. In fact, Portugal did it and saw a great decrease in both drug abuse and violence. Others will say that young people will be tempted to try drugs if they are made legal. But isn't it true that those who will try drugs will probably try them *anyway*? So, the question is: Will they try them safely with product that has quality control, purchasing them without violence, buy them from a store, etc.? Or, will they try them the way things are now with heroin that is mixed with rat poison, and possibly get killed buying from some dealer in an alley? Part of the allure of drugs is that they are illegal. And because most of the violence is because they are illegal, the ones who suffer the most are the kids. We could significantly curb crime just by making drugs safe and legal.

One of the biggest objections I hear to this approach is the denial by those who have never had to deal with the drug issue personally. They will usually say "Never my kids." Or they will say that this problem is because parents failed in some way. But I know parents of kids who were addicted to heroin and those parents were pastors, school teachers, highly educated people with doctorate degrees, missionaries, cops, and just about every other walk of life. Denial is simply lying to yourself. Yes, it can happen to you. And it seems more and more lately, it is happening to a wider cross section of society. The junkie is no longer some derelict in an alleyway sticking a needle in his arm. He is now your son or daughter doing it in the bedroom of your middle class home.

Finally, some will say that certain drugs cause people to act violently. But I am left to wonder if that is because some of those drugs are being made in basements where nobody know what is in them? I am also wondering whether they are cheap replacements to some of the more expensive drugs on the street. If drugs were manufactured using industry standards, the purity and consistency would be known. When you buy a bottle of Tylenol in New York City or in Los Angeles, you know you are getting the same stuff. There is no question about potency or dosage. If drugs were treated similarly, the effects would be better known. Studies could be done. Treatment programs would be more effective. But the best part is that the drug dealers, street violence, beheadings in Mexico, DEA agents and cops breaking down doors in the middle of the night shooting the dog or grandma, kids without fathers, gang members killing over turf, 2,000,000 people in jail--much of that will vanish.

# War on War

As Christians we ought to advocate for staying out of foreign wars. There is little room for war in the New Testament and Jesus never endorses it. That doesn't mean that I am a pacifist. I believe that sometimes the only course of action that remains to end evil is war. But it should be done hesitantly and only when left with no other option.

The USA has had a one hundred plus year history of getting involved in foreign wars that have sent our sons and daughters to their graves or has brought them back maimed for life with no real American interests at stake. I ask you, truly, would you willingly send your son or your daughter to die in Vietnam to fight the communists? What about to the Korean peninsula to fight them there? Are your children's lives worth that? I am not re-litigating our involvement in those wars and I believe those who went were all heroes. I also believe that our presidents acted in what they believed to be the most prudent way forward. But we can either learn the lesson in retrospect or we can keep making the same mistakes.

Let's face it. The USA has wasted many of our kids' lives, trillions of our tax dollars, and much of our good reputation around the world fighting wars that we didn't belong in. Our kids have fought and died valiantly. Many of them died as heroes. We can never repay their sacrifice. But we also can never replace them at the dinner table. We have the best armed forces ever to walk the face of this earth. But we don't need to send them to places that are not in our own best interests. And, when we *do* send them, it ought to be because our nation is at real risk or because we have been genuinely attacked. (I say genuinely because the Spanish-American War and possibly WW I were based on questionable premises.)

This nation is being pushed to keep building its war machine. On January 17, 1961 departing President Dwight Eisenhower warned the country that a "Military Industrial Complex" was dangerously pushing the United States towards wars. These are our own domestic companies that push the military to keep upgrading, keep spending, keep advancing our capabilities. But, if we are honest about ourselves and about human nature, having all of that hardware tempts us to use it. When we blow up a bomb that costs $1 million, that money is wasted forever. If we built a road with it, or a school, or helped 20 kids go to college, wouldn't that be money better spent?

In his book, 1984, George Orwell wrote these haunting words, "The essential act of war is destruction, not necessarily of human lives, but of the products of human labour. War is a way of shattering to pieces, or pouring into the stratosphere, or sinking in the depths of the sea, materials which might otherwise be used to make the masses too comfortable, and hence, in the long run, too intelligent. Even when weapons of war are not actually destroyed, their manufacture is still a convenient way of expending labour power without producing anything that can be consumed."

Perhaps having read Orwell's book, which was only written a few years earlier, the great World War II military general Dwight Eisenhower would give a speech on April 16, 1953 to the American Society of Newspaper Editors. In that speech he said the following:

"Every gun that is made, every warship launched, every rocket fired signifies, in the final sense, a theft from those who hunger and are not fed, those who are cold and not clothed. This world in arms is not spending money alone. It is spending the sweat of its laborers, the genius of its scientists, the hopes of its children...

The cost of one modern heavy bomber is this: a modern brick school in more than 30 cities. It is two electric power plants, each serving a town of 60,000 population. It is two fine, fully equipped hospitals. It is some fifty miles of concrete pavement. We pay for a single fighter with a half-million bushels of wheat. We pay for a single destroyer with new homes that could have housed more than 8,000 people...

This is not a way of life at all in any true sense. Under the cloud of threatening war, it is humanity hanging from a cross of iron."

Ponder those words. The USA needs to rethink its war posturing. We need to stay out of foreign wars and only go to war when our people or land are directly at risk or attacked. Anything more than that only invites pain and heart-ache to the American people. Our alliances through NATO only drag us into wars that we don't belong fighting. We have become the world's police and other nations don't give anywhere near the money or blood that we do. Why should we continue in that pursuit?

Consider these three quotes from Thomas Paine who was one of the great orators of the American Revolution,

"To establish any mode to abolish war, however advantageous it might be to Nations, would be to take from such Government the most lucrative of its branches."

"He who is the author of a war lets loose the whole contagion of hell and opens a vein that bleeds a nation to death."

"War involves in its progress such a train of unforeseen circumstances that no human wisdom can calculate the end; it has but one thing certain, and that is to increase taxes."

Paine was right. War stinks and we should avoid it as much as possible. If I were to make one exception to this rule it would be the exception of a humanitarian war effort. If we, the greatest world power, cannot use our military to stop genocides, then we don't deserve that station on earth's stage. Jesus said that to whom much is given, much shall be required. But the USA simply cannot be the world's policeman. We should rather be as those who stop genocides and then quickly leave the battlefield.

If we were to take this seriously, it would also mean that we close down our numerous military bases in foreign lands. Think about it: Why do we still occupy Germany nearly three quarters of a century after the Second World War? Why do we still occupy Japan? Or, North Korea? The wars that got us there are long over. Why do we have bases all over the world? The people that live in those countries see the face of America as a a military power instead of a friendly, peace-loving people. The reason we stay in these places is to have strategic places around the earth to deploy military assets anytime there is a need. This goes along with our function of being the world's police. But I must question why we are the world's police? Why must it be hard-working Americans who have to always pay when there is trouble in a far away land? Our national debt is at $20 trillion and rising daily. We are broke and we are being taken advantage of by the world's other governments. While they are giving their people nationalized healthcare, free tuition, all sorts of socialist welfare, they are not paying for their own defense or their part in being in NATO because they know that the USA will always fill that void. The money they are saving is going to their socialism. I am not advocating we do the same. But the money we save if we back off can help Americans live better lives and not be as stressed paying their bills.

The military bases we have all over the world cost lots of money to operate. They take our military to foreign lands, away from their families and lives. Many of them are relics from a day when the US and Soviet Union were in the cold war. That war ended 20 years ago. Others are left overs from previous wars. If we were to cut these bases and focus on our homeland, we could come close to solving the US deficit! There is no need for these bases except to promote a militarism around the world. We have almost 800 military bases around the world that are currently in operation. Every one of them costs taxpayers many millions of dollars.


## A Clash of Civilizations

As  follower of Jesus, I hate war and I wish there would never be another war. But I know that is a dream. As long as man seeks power over his fellow man, there will be "wars and rumors of wars" (i.e., Matthew 24:6) till Jesus comes.

In the 1930's and early 1940's, Hitler wanted to rule the world. He invaded and made advances into neighboring countries with his armies, imposing his megalomaniacal vision upon them. A part of that strategy was "the final solution", the extermination of Jews and other "undesirables" from the land. It's hard for anyone to not see that we have a parallel situation going on in the Middle East today. Radical Sunni Muslims seeking to impose a global caliphate with Sharia law are invading countries and imposing their similar megalomaniacal vision upon them. They, too, wish to exterminate Jews. But add to that their desire to kill Christians, Hindus, Buddhists, and even other non-conforming Shiite Muslims.

In hindsight, most of us wish we had never entered Iraq. It took a brutal dictator to keep that region stable. A horde of brutal dictators is now seeking to do the same. But they want to impose it on the whole world. Even now they have infiltrated the US and other Westernized nations and are planning the strategy for their vision.

The approach that President Obama's administration took to that threat was to hug them and play kissy-kissy with them. He was living in absolute delusional denial of the very real and growing existential threat we faced. He believed if we just treat them nice that they will be our friends. He was blinded by his liberal humanistic ideology that believes all people are basically good. But human history shows us that they aren't. And he had not learned its lessons and was condemning us to repeat its mistakes. Trump's approach reversed that delusional self-sacrificial hope for peace and is taking the correct tact of eliminating the threat. In this case, we have both a national interest because ISIS has radicalized people on our soil who have carried out attacks, and a humanitarian interest after seeing what they did to the Syrian and Iraqi people.

I was not a big fan of George W. Bush, but he was right about the global war on terrorism. He may have been wrong in some instances as to how it should be executed—getting us involved in Iraq being the prime example. But be very sure that we are in that war. And we will either fight it, or we will wake up one day and find the "Barbarians at the gates". And then it will be too late. "And woe unto them that are with child, and to them that give suck in those days!"

Repeat: I Hate War

I really do hate war. But we are in one that amounts to a clash of civilizations--whether we like it or not, whether President Obama believed it or not, whether Trump fights it or not, or whether it fits your world-view or not. God help us. War is a very serious thing and we ought to involve ourselves in it only when *not* doing so will result in harm to our homeland or infringe on our liberties and way of life. But we should do it with dread, fear, and trepidation.

So, when we do have to fight a war, we should also fight any war that we get involved in to win. We cannot have rules of engagement that tie our soldiers' hands behind their backs. We should give the authority for generals to do whatever is necessary, by whatever means necessary to win. Our experience in Iraq and Afghanistan should have taught us something. If we went into Afghanistan with overwhelming and merciless force using the power that the USA has just short of nuclear weapons and turned that place into a virtual parking lot, the war would have lasted perhaps a month or so. Most of the American lives that we lost would probably have been saved. Few of our soldiers would come back home with missing limbs, and we would be at peace. There is no mercy, there is no kindness, there is no nice way to fight a war. We kill people and break things. That is how it is won.

I have heard some argue that we are creating more enemies by occupying a country like Afghanistan. I think there is some truth to that. Think about the fact that there are children who were born when we entered that country in 2001 that are now approaching fighting age. Those kids have only known war all their lives. Do you think we've won their hearts and minds? Do you think these "kinder, gentler" wars have shown them mercy? If we had gone in there back in 2001 and overwhelmed them with the type of force I just spoke of, yes there would have been many more initial casualties on their part. But the war would have ended quickly and Afghanistan would be rebuilt by now. That, it seems, would have been far more merciful than this endless war which is ravaging these people and gives them no hope, no perspective, no purpose other than to either fight or survive.

Why do I take such a strong stand against war? Because I am a parent of five beautiful kids and a grandparent of nine (soon to be ten) grandkids. There is no comfort that we can bring to a mother who spent twenty years in the prime of her life pouring her heart and soul into raising a son for him to be killed in a foreign war for no real benefit to the USA. And can we explain to her how our rules of engagement would not allow him to shoot his enemy even though they shot him? Would that give her some solace? And what will we do to comfort this mother who will never have grandchildren, who will not dance with her son at his wedding, and who will never again feel his embrace? Will our politicians flatter his grave with flowers, flags, and 21-gun salutes?

Will that somehow lend succor this mother's empty embrace? How arrogantly presumptuous to even think so.

And won't that dead soldier's absence be felt long after the government hands his widow the folded flag? The daughter whose cheek will go unkissed for the rest of her life, the wife who will sleep alone and raise her kids alone, the daughter who will not have her father to give her away at her wedding, and the son who will never go fishing with his dad. Will they be satisfied? Will their joy be replenished with a folded flag?

---

*Generals gathered in their masses,*
*Just like witches at black masses.*
*Evil minds that plot destruction,*
*Sorcerer of death's construction.*
*In the fields the bodies burning,*
*As the war machine keeps turning.*
*Death and hatred to mankind,*
*Poisoning their brainwashed minds*
*...Oh Lord, yeah!*

*Politicians hide themselves away*
*They only started the war*
*Why should they go out to fight?*
*They leave that role to the poor.*

*Time will tell on their power minds*
*Making war just for fun*
*Treating people just like pawns in chess*
*Wait till their judgment day comes, yeah!*

*Now in darkness, world stops turning,*
*Ashes where the bodies burning.*
*No more war pigs have the power,*
*Hand of God has struck the hour.*
*Day of judgment, God is calling,*
*On their knees the war pigs crawling.*
*Begging mercy for their sins,*
*Satan, laughing, spreads his wings*
*...Oh Lord, yeah!*
~~~~~War Pigs, Black Sabbath

---
~~~~~

# Socialism and Economics

About 30 years ago I had the stark realization that if I was going to depend on others for my livelihood, I would live a life of dependency and certain disappointment. At the time I worked for a major oil company which was treating me very well. In fact, I have never since had the benefits and stability that I had back then. However, since leaving that company, I have also been mostly able to live the life that I want. I have enjoyed the liberty to make my own hours, to go where I want and when I want, to think my own thoughts and to live free. There is a price you pay that can't always be measured in dollars when you work for someone or when you depend on others for your survival. This is true of those who work a job. This is also true of those who depend on entitlements.

The vision that some of the Founding Fathers had--particularly Thomas Jefferson--was that people would own their own land and farm it or do as they wished, sustaining their lives by their own efforts. The yeoman farmers (as they were called) were to be the building blocks of this country. Your food, your clothing, your basic needs were met by your own hands or by the sale of the goods you produced which provided the money to buy the things that you couldn't produce. That life, though it may have seemed difficult by today's standards, actually allowed the USA to eventually become the world's strongest economy. The people of the world heard stories that gold was to be found on the streets. And, in some sense, that was true because we became the cradle of the industrial revolution. American rugged individualism was not just a phrase in history books, but a way of life that wrought the success we enjoyed as a nation.

As I look at the current state of this country, I find that government has supplanted that way of life with a new "progressive vision" which has had the effect of discouraging independence and encouraging dependence. It has taken away the virtue of individuals contributing to the overall economy by luring people into cities to seek employment from non-existent employers.

Money is now needed for every aspect of life, not just things you cannot provide for yourself. Food is being grown by large corporate concerns which do it more efficiently, but also feed us things that we wouldn't want to eat. And those concerns are recipients of corporate welfare in exchange for government control over much of their production. We are being trained to be dependent on a system that is clearly failing.

If I could give anyone advice today, it would be to do whatever you can to become less dependent the system. You may not have a lucrative pension (which may not be there anyway). You may not have great health insurance or dental insurance. But you will be working toward attaining the freedom to live your own life as you see fit. You will work toward your own pursuit of happiness. In some ways, the Amish have it right. You may not be able to completely remove yourself unless you go live in a cabin in Montana. But you will find the freedom that you didn't enjoy before to be liberating to your soul and the simpler life to be more fulfilling.

Why spend your life working hard in this system to make money to attain the material things only to lose your own soul, to lose your children, to lose your marriage? Prosperity is good. But not at the cost of being a slave to the machine. Jesus asked "What shall it profit a man if he gain the world and lose his own soul? Or, what shall a man give in exchange for his soul?" (Mark 8:36-37). We are selling our souls, hour by hour, day by day, week after week and year after year, simply that we might live. There is more to life than this.


Feeling "the Bern"
A Modern Parable of Socialist Reasoning


A hard working plumber finally gets his time completed as an apprentice. He'd worked hard to learn the trade, learned the business, took the test and now has a state license to be a plumbing contractor. He had saved as much money as he could, but he needed more to get his business going. Taking the risk of possibly losing it all, but believing in himself, he borrows $50,000 against his home to buy a plumbing truck and some of the more expensive tools.

After five years of hard work and doing exceptional work to build a business, it pays off and he repays the entire loan. He leaves his house at 7 a.m. and returns home sometimes as late as 8 p.m. and works six days a week, taking off very few holidays. But he's been able to hire a couple of apprentices himself and eventually he buys his wife that Mercedes Benz she's always wanted.  After fifteen years of marriage they finally decide to go on the honeymoon that they have never had. They drive their new Mercedes all the way down to Key West and spend a week eating well, living well, enjoying the music, the atmosphere and the island life.

In one instance, the Mercedes pulls up and parks in front of a nice restaurant and out comes the plumber and his wife. A Bernie Sanders supporter happens to be their waiter that night and he thinks to himself that it is unfair this man and his wife can pull up in a new Mercedes and eat filet minion while the waiter is struggling to make tips to pay his rent and eat Ramon Noodles. Not only that, but he has $75,000 in student loans for his degree in Oceanography and he can't even find a job in his field. But he knows that the vision of a guy like Socialist Vermont Senator and presidential candidate Bernie Sanders will make it so that these rich people will have to pay their fair share.

This is the thinking that is going on in the minds of these young socialist supporters. The reason so many young people followed him during the 2016 presidential election is that they don't really have all the facts concerning socialism. Every year there is a new vintage of young minds that enter the colleges with a virtual tabula rasa (i.e., a "blank slate") who are taught selectively about liberal ideas. I say this because surveys confirm that the majority of college professors are liberals, tent toward socialism, and teach those ideas. This explains the 2016 Bernie phenomenon well.

But this type of thinking is so wrong and tragic, really, on many levels. The story of the plumber can be repeated thousands of times across the country every day. Most people did not get their lives handed to them. And those that work hard and take the risks are often rewarded, not because fate looked pleasantly down upon them, but because self-determination and hard work usually pays off— if not at first, then eventually.

We've really created an economic monster with government interventions in the marketplace. Instead of seeking to redistribute people's hard work and homogenize the "wealth distribution" through socialism by unfair taxation, the government should only spend what it takes in and tax policy should be fair to the laborers and entrepreneurs. But the socialist impulses in the ambitious US government has brought it to the habit of spending more than it receives from revenues because it has taken upon itself the responsibility of too much social welfare. The politicians are using the tax revenues to buy votes. And when their spending exceeds revenues, they borrow the money by issuing bonds. The issuance of bonds in one year is called the deficit and it is the amount of money the government overspent in that year. Just to put this in perspective, the US government spent about $1 trillion for the first time ever in 1990. Less than twenty years later, the federal deficit—the overspending, not the budget-- during the first several years of the Obama administration had averaged around $1.3 trillion each year! These deficits get added to the national debt, which is the total of all our deficits from all the previous years. The national debt as of the writing of this book is nearly $20 trillion.

Why should this bother us? Simply because this money will be repaid by future generation--your kids and grandkids. Spending borrowed money means that you are living today with future earnings, jeopardizing your future living standard because of the debt you will be repaying for today's expenses. But since we are talking about a country and not an individual, a country can theoretically keep borrowing money into the future because old people are replaced with younger people. So we just make the minimum payments (sort of like paying interest only on your credit card) and continue to push the debt forward to the next generation of workers, adding to it every year.

The outcome of this is obvious. One day we will reach our debt limit--not as the congress sets it periodically, but as the math stops working. When the interest payments start to eat up so much of our revenue that the government can't pay the rest of its expenses, we will have a budgetary and monetary crisis which will cause this nation to go the way of the Weimar Republic or Zimbabwe. Austerity measures will not work.

Some have drawn the comparison to what happened to Greece and Spain in the 2010's. But it will actually be far worse because they had the rest of the European Union to bail them out. The US will have nobody to bail us out because we *are* the world's reserve currency. There will be social unrest and a possible collapse of our government. That scenario often gives rise to a dictatorship--all in the name of restoring law and order. Is this the future you want for your kids?

And sadly, much of the borrowed money is going to waste supporting socialist programs, unnecessary wars, and bloated government bureaucracies, not to mention that the working class are being burdened and taxed to death. Why are we sending money abroad to nations that hate us? Why are we policing the whole world? Why are we funding research for shrimp running on a miniature treadmill? That is not a joke. We really did waste tax money on it. And other stupid things?

Despite what you hear in liberal news outlets, the vast majority of our federal dollars are spent on social programs. So why are we allowing able-bodied people to make a lifestyle choice to stay home and collect welfare, section 8 housing vouchers, energy assistance, medicaid, food stamps, EBT cards, free cell phones, etc.? The entitlement programs make up the lion's share of the budget and the lion's share of waste and abuse in the federal budget. Those who need help should be put on a limit. It should be uncomfortable to stay home. It shouldn't be a viable lifestyle choice. There are many ways to get entitlement recipients to be productive citizens through workfare or community service vouchers. We can have cleaner streets, janitorial services in public buildings, clerical help, even some volunteerism in various organizations that do good works in the community. Why should we waste such a valuable resource by paying them to sit home and watch Jerry Springer?

The bottom line is simple: Let the government ONLY spend what it takes in and reform the so-called "social safety net programs."

While we are talking about budget deficits, we should also look to end ALL corporate welfare and subsidies. The nation spends billions of dollars to prop up certain industries. Without this corporate welfare, the free market would pick the winners and losers based on the economic viability of any given company and the free market. Why should the American taxpayer give money to Solyndra (a failed "green energy" company) or to GM and Chrysler? Why should the taxpayer give many thousands of dollars to subsidize electric cars which are bought primarily by wealthy people trying to portray themselves as "green warriors"? There is no reason for the government to prop up companies that often fail and leave taxpayers holding the bag. Why should the government pay some farmers to NOT produce? Why should the government create an artificial demand for corn by requiring that ethanol be mixed into gasoline— something which has caused many mechanical problems in our vehicles? All of these create market distortions which pick winners and losers and hide the *real* price of goods. Many times these subsidies are used to reward political donors and friends of the politically connected. The CATO Institute did a study on corporate welfare during the George Bush Jr. administration and found that we were spending $92 billion in 2006. That amount must be well north of $100 billion today. And much of that money went to companies like IBM, Boeing, and GE.

While we are giving money to corporations and treating certain industries with favor, the taxpayers are on the hook for higher taxes and the future generations have nearly $20 trillion in national debt to pay.

Making matters worse, during the 2008 financial market meltdown, in the great wisdom of the Bush and Obama administrations, we bailed out hundreds of banks. We bailed out investment firms. We bailed out mortgage firms. We bailed out insurance companies like AIG. All of this bail out money went to the very people that created that mess and the government was complicit and even actively participating in creating the mess.

At the same time, many people ended up losing their homes because it was those very companies that made the poor investment decisions and who lobbied congress to change the rules. Furthermore, the government distorted the housing industry by pushing bankers to loan money to unqualified buyers, driving the prices of homes up and the stability of the financial markets down. The financial disaster that we are now in was mostly the result of government involving itself in the mortgage market by giving Fanny Mae and Freddie Mac the implied government backing which inevitably lead them to be reckless with their lending practices. People were losing their homes because, like it or not, the free market will always correct distortions one way or another.

Have we learned anything? Both corporate socialism and individual socialism have been abysmal failures as a matter of policy. It is high time the government stick with the limitations that are enumerated in our Constitution and get out of the marketplace. Here are those enumerated powers as quoted from the US Constitution:

The Congress shall have Power To lay and collect Taxes, Duties, Imposts and Excises, to pay the Debts and provide for the common Defense and general Welfare of the United States; but all Duties, Imposts and Excises shall be uniform throughout the United States;

To borrow on the credit of the United States;

To regulate Commerce with foreign Nations, and among the several States, and with the Indian Tribes;

To establish a uniform Rule of Naturalization, and uniform Laws on the subject of Bankruptcies throughout the United States;

To coin Money, regulate the Value thereof, and of foreign Coin, and fix the Standard of Weights and Measures;

To provide for the Punishment of counterfeiting the Securities and current Coin of the United States;

To establish Post Offices and Post Roads;

To promote the Progress of Science and useful Arts, by securing for limited Times to Authors and Inventors the exclusive Right to their respective Writings and Discoveries;

To constitute Tribunals inferior to the supreme Court;

To define and punish Piracies and Felonies committed on the high Seas, and Offenses against the Law of Nations;

To declare War, grant Letters of Marque and Reprisal, and make Rules concerning Captures on Land and Water;

To raise and support Armies, but no Appropriation of Money to that Use shall be for a longer Term than two Years;

To provide and maintain a Navy;

To make Rules for the Government and Regulation of the land and naval Forces;

118

To provide for calling forth the Militia to execute the Laws of the Union, suppress Insurrections and repel Invasions;

To provide for organizing, arming, and disciplining, the Militia, and for governing such Part of them as may be employed in the Service of the United States, reserving to the States respectively, the Appointment of the Officers, and the Authority of training the Militia according to the discipline prescribed by Congress;

To exercise exclusive Legislation in all Cases whatsoever, over such District (not exceeding ten Miles square) as may, by Cession of particular States, and the acceptance of Congress, become the Seat of the Government of the United States, and to exercise like Authority over all Places purchased by the Consent of the Legislature of the State in which the Same shall be, for the Erection of Forts, Magazines, Arsenals, dock-Yards, and other needful Buildings; And

To make all Laws which shall be necessary and proper for carrying into Execution the foregoing Powers, and all other Powers vested by this Constitution in the Government of the United States, or in any Department or Officer thereof.
~~~~~Article I, Section 8 of the United States Constitution
~~~~~

## What is Labor?

I want to close this chapter with my view of labor. My view of things is usually brutally honest and that sometimes grates on people the wrong way. But I try to think about things as objectively as I can. So when I write something like this, it usually invokes (or provokes) responses in people that are visceral and not necessarily thought out. You have seen so far in this book that much of what I write comes down to economic policies or government intrusions into our liberties. But a person who thinks through these issues may be forced to admit the truth about my conclusions because they are not necessarily motivated by politics but by observation and common sense.

With that said, I want to explain how I see labor. In modern times, the greatest economic asset we have to participate in the economy is our own labor. Labor can be seen as small increments of my life that I am willing to sell for a given price. We only have so many of them before they run out AND only a portion of them are even "sellable." Think about that this way: Very few 0-12 year olds can sell their time. Those that do are usually child actors or models. By the time you hit about 13 you *might* be able to sell your time to people who need a youthful hand cutting grass, doing chores or being a "go-fer." At around 16 you can get a minimum wage entry-level job that *ought* to be your gateway into the labor force. Now, on the other end of that spectrum, by the time you're in your 50's your marketability begins to decline as rapidly as your health. But the *key* there is your brain. If you are educated and have certain mastery of skills, you can work into your 80's if you choose to. This is *important* for young people to know and should encourage them to go to school for higher education or to learn a marketable skill that has low impact on your body.

So, you could say that in my view, laborers are a form of "prostitutes" that sell their lives in one hour increments to the highest bidders. When they have no useful life left to sell (to those who are bidding), they are thrown away like garbage. Sadly, afterwards, often even their own families often won't care for them and they may end up in a nursing home or in squalor. Therefore, they need to make sure that they provide for themselves in their old age. This is especially true because the "benevolent hand of the government" is not always reliable and governments are transient on the world stage of history.

Thinking about labor this way is another reason why we need to stop the intrusive hand of government from taking from the laborers and, instead, allowing them to live well, support their families and save for their golden years. But hidden taxes, mandates, costs, confiscations, etc. make it that saving money today is almost impossible. This is also why home ownership is falling. According to a study done by National Foundation for Credit Counseling most Americans can't even sustain a $1000 hit to their life in an emergency. Taxing labor has only been going on about a hundred years. At first it didn't have a great effect on people's lives. It does does so increasingly now.

While we are on this subject I want to offer one more piece of advice: Make your money work for you. You should try to live below your income level when you are young and save all you can. Despite the fact that the US government is stealing the value of your savings by monetary policy, do it anyway. At some point you can convert those savings into an investment. Buy a home. Buy a rental property. Start a business. Invest in a diversified mutual fund. If you live by this rule, you will do well in your old age. I believe that a hard-working person who saves his money and doesn't "waste his substance with riotous living" (i.e., the Prodigal son, Luke 15:13) will do well for himself and his family.

# Global Warming

One the this big issues confronting us in the 21st century is the "Climate Change" debate. There are many who are on the liberal side of the aisle that believe this is an existential threat to the future of life on this planet. I know people who have said that they will not have children because they do not wish to contribute to the earth's desecration by mankind. In their sincerely held beliefs, they hold that mankind has been a scourge to this earth and that the fewer people on the planet, the better for its future prospects.

So, with the dire warnings of impending extinction, I believe it is legitimate to ask why are we still smashing 100+ year old cold records, snow records, ice records around the globe? If one considers himself a scientifically-minded person, doesn't that give you even a little pause? The core of this global warming theory is challenged by just that fact because if the globe is (as a whole) warming, these broken records should *not* be happening globally. But the broken records seem to be dispersed all over the planet. We're not talking about isolated places. Records keep getting broken in both hemispheres and in all continents. And, while it is true that they are also being broken in warming, too, what does the whole amount to? Honestly.

In November of 2009, a batch of emails that were hacked from East Anglia University global warming researchers showed that there was substantial manipulation of temperature data and its proxies in order to hide the fact that global warming had taken a fairly long hiatus. There appears to have been a subsequent cover up by investigators who are policing their own—sort of like police departments who investigate cops shooting citizens and seldom find anything wrong. A subsequent study done of the temperature data shows that it has been manipulated to demonstrate an up trend in what was actually flat to down trend in many cases.

Add to this a comprehensive study done by Anthony Watts, a seasoned meteorologist and researcher, that showed many of the thermometers used by NOAA "have been compromised by encroachment of artificial surfaces like concrete, asphalt, and heat sources like air conditioner exhausts."

Instead of having the liberals constantly resort to name calling and labeling people like me a "denier", I am asking for intellectual honesty in this debate and I seldom get it. Ad hominem attacks don't answer the issues. But they are a useful tool to convince the unthinking to just go along with the agenda because name-calling prompts a visceral response instead of an intellectual one.

As I have looked at this issue over many years, there are several issues I have a problem with when talking to "Global Warmers." The first is the baseline they use to determine warming. Here is the NOAA chart that most people  will agree is the one climate scientists use.

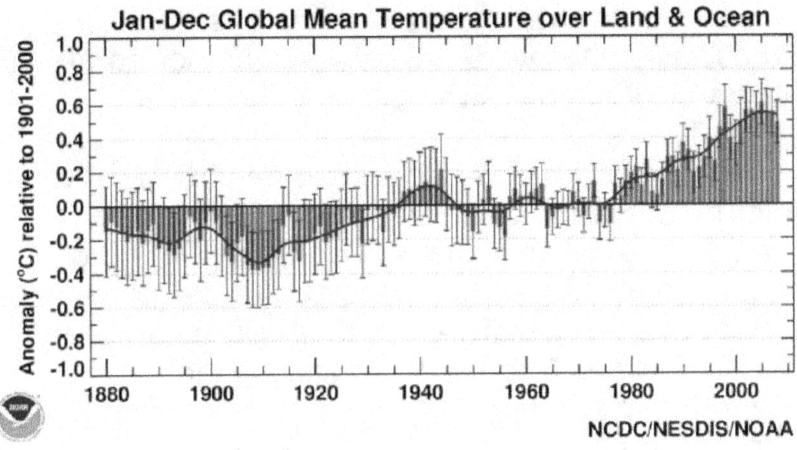



The temperature baseline is established by approximately 130 years of data. But it is a legitimate question to ask why is that 130 years of data the standard by which to judge the warming? The warming may be worse or better if we had longer data set. The fact that this is the only data we have shouldn't then be the reason to declare something is amiss. Something may be. But something also may not be.

Add to that the unreliability of the older data, and you are left to wonder whether those extreme cold and hot temps were valid a century ago? Let's also not forget that the accuracy of thermometers for weather (as compared to laboratory thermometers) is generally about ±1° but we have an argument about global warming of less than that 1°! So the data used to compile this argument actually exceeds the reliability of the instruments that measure it. At this point one must ask whether this really science or some form of religious faith?

The second issue is about the magnitude of the actual deviation from the mean global temperature. On a planet--and keep in mind that the issue here is purported to be global--that sees temperatures that range from nearly -129 degrees F to +134 degrees F, an "anomaly" of even 1° C± (which is more than has been actually recorded) seems statistically insignificant, representing around 1/250th deviation from that scale. Is that as significant as they are making it out to be?

The third issue is more about the core of their argument, which is the correlation of CO2 to an alleged "anthropocentric global warming". The Mauna Loa observatory (which is the climate science standard) has recorded steadily increasing levels of CO2 since 1960 when it first started to be measured. The amount of CO2 in the total atmosphere is measured in PPM (parts per million). That measurement started at approximately 315 ppm and is now about 405 ppm--a 25% increase in those nearly 60 years. Yet the temperature has not increased by any such proportions and that immediately raises the mathematical question whether there even *is* a statistical correlation of temperature to CO2. A related question might be if there *is* correlation, does it start to take effect at higher levels since it still doesn't appear to have meaningfully done so at these levels? I ask these questions because as a philosophy student I did also take classes in logic and statistics and it would appear that this is an elephant in the room. Do we REALLY believe that an increase of about .01% in atmospheric CO2 is going to warm the entire globe and create the catastrophe that is being peddled by the global warming faithful?

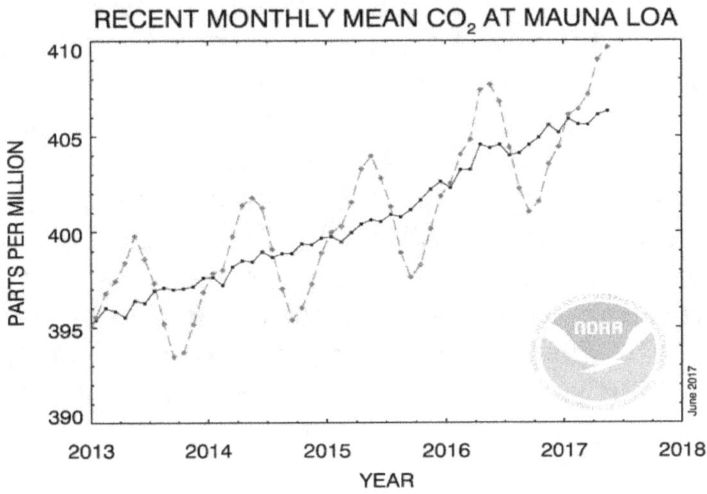


Maybe those who just spout off the talking points haven't delved into it like me here. But consider these things and know that there are many more things that bother me about this.

The anecdotal evidence that I have seen, taken together, for this entire "Holocene Epoch" shows a vacillation in temperatures over the written portion of history (around 3000 BC to the present.). A study of European vineyard records shows harvests as early as September and as late as November. This is anecdotal, but an implicit proxy about climate variableness.

The Viking Era farming in Greenland during the Middle Ages which is well known and documented but currently impossible tells another story of temperate times in the past. There are many other things that ought to be looked at such as the period known as the Medieval Climate Optimum which some historians say took us out of the dark ages and gave rise to the Renaissance. Yet, the Global Warming faithful still *insist* that the earth is warmer today despite that evidence. If that alone is not a blindness of theory over facts, then I suppose nothing is. This is just confirmation bias bordering on a religious cult. The Roman period around the time of Christ, the building of the Egyptian Pyramids and the Golden age of Greece all also anecdotally speak of similar warmer periods on earth.

On the other side of that coin, depictions of George Washington crossing the Delaware River show ice on the river. Yet the Delaware seldom gets meaningfully iced over. Was that a colder period on earth? Many say yes and have termed it a mini ice age.

I should also mention that there is very little "for profit" climatology. In fact, I've never seen any--just forecasting the weather which is not the same thing. All funding for climate study comes from the government. If you know of any other, please let me know because I've never seen it. This all being true, then let's make a point about the sociology of academic climate science. You can't expect to get funding from the government for anything that may negate the narrative the government bureaucrats are trying to push. Any "rebels" who may find contrary data are immediately shut out of the research for fear of risking the government funding. The government teat is big and supplies endless money to those who are obedient and persist in feeding the narrative. This corrupts the science and creates an atmosphere in academia that stifles honesty. This is now an academic field with a theory in search of supporting data. Further, you can't expect to get tenure from the tenure-givers if you fall out of line.

Let me also add another interesting dimension to this debate here: Coal and oil represent the sequestration of CO2 by plants and animals that lived many years ago. By whatever processes (some of them are still debated) they were buried quickly enough to prevent the usual process which would have allowed those gases to escape as a result of decomposition and instead were buried in an anaerobic environment which let them form oil or coal.

The burning of these fossil fuels, then, can be seen as a reversal of that sequestration process. That, along with the corals and other limestones which also sequester CO2 are a natural process over many centuries and millennia. So, in effect, the atmospheric CO2 remains within a range and we are actually at a lower point historically than we likely are over the earth's history. I believe the ice core samples taken around the globe show that to be the case. But some have played with that data, too. There were periods in the past where the CO2 levels are ten times what they are today.

Destroying Species

Many have said that this warming is destroying the planet and species are dying off. But I don't think we are destroying species at any greater rate than they have been going into extinction naturally. I believe the fossil record demonstrates this aptly. I also believe that self-justification plays into these discussions because nobody wants to believe that their job, their degree, or their research has no relevance. We want to feel like our lives are important and a person who spends four years or longer studying these things will be hesitant to surrender on the issue.

We humans have this obsession with keeping things static--as if somehow we even have the ability to do that on a macro-scale. We don't. And there is no amount of money--which represents human labor converted into fiat-- that will stop the planet from warming or cooling. Only a megalomaniacal group of ideologically driven "scientists" can arrive at the obscene conclusions that some of these have. The planet's temperatures will not obey no matter how much money we throw at it. We can't bribe the clouds.

Lest anyone get the wrong impression of what I am saying here, let me say clearly that I am by nature a preservationist. I am an environmentalist. I have five children and nine grandchildren and certainly more to look forward to. So, when someone looks at the arguments that I am making here, I hope they realize that I am not speaking out of some theoretical basis, but from the reality of life. To lay upon my kids and grandkids the burden of these proposed environmental fixes, which will do virtually nothing, yet sap billions and even trillions of dollars from my kids' already dismal looking future, is immoral and even evil.

I am not convinced that there has been much meaningful global warming over the last one hundred years. I am not convinced that whatever bit there has been necessarily has an anthropocentric cause. And I am not convinced that the entirety of industrial revolution has done any lasting harm to the environment-- even though in the near term there have been many ugly incidents and bad practices which I am glad have been corrected.

What few people in this debate want to see is that science is science and politics is politics. Rigorous science depends not on ideology, but on a spirit of honest inquiry and robust debate. Actual empirical evidence must supplant theory and proxy evidence. Skepticism and falsification must preside over working theories if the science is going to be real and accepted. Disproof of working theories cannot be viewed with disdain and disbelief. But *that* is what the current environment of Global Warming is all about.

Truthfully, burning fossil fuels may be doing some short term "harm" to the environment and warming may possibly be the slightest part of that (though I have my doubts). But if we were to absolutely *stop* burning fossil fuels today, to the extent that we have done any "harm", it would disappear in a matter of a few years. However, if we were to stop today we'd also greatly reduce the standard of living in the world—with the poorest people suffering the most because the wealthy have the means to compensate with other methods. That is the honest answer to this debate.

What about the Science?

Of course, I should also ask "What could possibly be wrong with modern science?" The hard push to get government funding will always give the government the outcome it wants. I am seeing that much modern science is simply predetermined conclusions waiting for confirmation studies. Global warming may be the ultimate example of this.

Unfortunately, the "science" also abuses kids who enter fields believing they'll be able to just study stuff all their life. College professors apply for money from the government to study a species of fish that some congressman wants protected because he got campaign money from an activist that wants the land which surrounds his estate kept from development. So they get enthusiastic kids to do much of the field work which dupes them into believing that is what marine biologists always do (I am not picking on them, they're just my example.)

How many poor kids are being duped into college degrees that are utterly worthless and makes them dependent on the largess of government? They are, indeed, a different class of welfare dependent people. Marine biologists, women's studies, African American studies, climatology (as opposed to meteorology), etc. who will probably never have gainful employment outside of government jobs or education. Maybe the marine biologist can get a private sector job at an aquarium or Sea World. The others? Not so much. How many places need people with a degree in women's studies?

Education has done these kids a disservice because their education is practically unmarketable. Do we need people with these degrees? Maybe a few. But should these become disciplines that attract many kids into a degree program? Ask the kids who have the degrees and are living in mom's basement working part time at Walmart and awaiting a call from one of the twenty jobs they applied for in government or education. Meanwhile they have $50,000 or more in student loans to get that wonderful degree. This is not theoretical. I've met quite a few in my life. They end up disheartened and working at jobs outside of their fields.

Fossil Fuels

Much of the global warming issue has to do with burning fossil fuels. But what about proposing some free market solutions to the issue of energy shortage and carbon footprint?

It is the function of Congress to pass laws and repeal laws. But they cannot touch the laws of economics because they are *higher* than congress and beyond their reach. It is the law of supply and demand that we are talking about when we say free market solutions to the energy shortage.

The laws of economics tell us that drilling for oil will create more supply. And it is a basic law of economics that higher supply means lower prices. But oftentimes the government's restrictions that have been placed on exploration has made it that oil is harder to find. This has sometimes helped to keep gasoline prices stubbornly high. And if gasoline was maybe a dollar cheaper, we would possibly not be in this general economic malaise because more money would be flowing through the economy creating and sustaining jobs instead of getting burned in our cars.

Think about it this way, the United States consumes a total of about seven billion barrels of oil in any given year. If gasoline was just a dollar less per gallon it would have meant about $250 billion more in people's pockets circulating in our domestic economy instead of much of it going overseas. This is because our energy policy is not sound. The overly zealous green movement has basically tried to take the US from gasoline to electric cars in one step which has encouraged higher gas prices and has kept us foreign oil dependent.

To his credit, President Obama did try to address the problem. But he listened to his leftist environmentalist ideologues whose real goal was carbon reduction *not* less oil dependence. For this reason his administration became bogged down with EPA rules that nearly strangled the economy. A free market approach would have kept oil cheaper while capitalist innovation would have kept working on a transition from oil to some other energy. This is the smart way forward and I am hopeful that the Trump administration will pursue that path.

In fact a few years ago T. Boone Pickens (one such capitalist) revealed a plan that he had been working on for better than a decade. He has built windmill farms for electricity while working on natural gas to use as a transportation fuel--a option which has unfortunately been shunned. Yet we have so much natural gas in this country that we have slowed down in extracting it. In the decade of the 2000's, natural gas prices had been running as high as $8, and even spiked over $13 once. But in the years following the fracking boom it has gone much lower and has even gone under $2 at times! This is because we have such an abundant supply here in the US and that is mostly because the government hasn't squashed production like they did oil. And because of the new fracking techniques we are getting an explosion of natural gas supply. That is how prices react to supply in a free market. If the price of oil did a similar thing, gasoline would be selling for under $1 right now. Pickens had offered a plan to take transportation fuel in the US from gasoline to natural gas as an intermediate step to some other form. But Obama's people shunned it for political reasons and because his donors and environmentalist buddies don't want us burning ANYTHING—oil, gasoline, natural gas, coal. Yet, this country has enough natural gas to last over 100 years!

As with anything else, always follow the money. If there is something out there that works and there is a demand for it, money will go to it naturally. Instead of the government shelling out taxpayer dollars on dreams and lies, we should let the free market solve the energy problem. We will never be able to run this country on windmills or solar. We would never be able to make enough electricity to do it. Yet, the government pays people to install solar in their homes. And those solar panels sometimes got a state subsidy as well. There are some people that I have spoken to who got their homes done in solar for free and they are now getting paid to have them on their roofs. How is that fair to people who rent instead of own? Or, to those who can't do that for various reasons? The unintended consequence has become the poor subsidizing the rich through taxation--especially in their electric bills.

The US also has enough coal to run the planet for over 100 years. The Obama administration's policies had made it that coal couldn't be used in the US for much longer. So, one by one, coal-fired electric generation plants were shutting down, and coal miners in Kentucky and West Virginia—these are the poor among us--were losing their jobs, and electricity is slowly climbing in price. The irony is that China is buying much of the coal that is still being mined. As they burn it instead of us, don't you think it still goes into the same air, on this same earth? Schizophrenic minds have a hard time with logic. Thankfully, Trump is reversing that trend and it is that type of thinking that got him elected.

It is a historic fact that when people discover ways to get cheap and plentiful energy, there is a corresponding boom in the economy which lifts that society into prosperity. The harnessing of rivers did it. The harnessing of gunpowder. Even the harnessing of slave labor in ancient empires. In modern times it was oil that gave us the Industrial Revolution and took us from relative peasantry to the lives we have today. The poorest among us live better than noblemen of times past--not in grandiosity, but in quality of life and convenience.

It's about being Rich

It is the wealthy that are funding much of the globalism and global warming hysteria that we have seen.  Yet they will not give up their yachts, airplanes, huge mansions and jet-set lifestyles. That is expected only of you. You see, global warming is not caused by the wealthy, the powerful, and the well-connected. No! Their massive carbon footprint is simply the cost of peddling the narrative--the preaching of the gospel of this non-Gaussian temperature spike and the fate of their goddess Gaia (the earth). It is you and I, oh unworthy peons, proles and minions that we are in their eyes, that must yield our comforts, mobility and 21st century lifestyle to the oligarchs of this plutocracy's demands. You, too, must worship the cult of Gaia as they command you and you must submit to their oracles--the IPCC and the priesthood of ordained climate scientists in white lab coats who subsist by the tithes brought them by government.

Of course, common sense and facts do not matter to these climate pantheists, who are willing to spare no expense on their goddess, Gaia--as long as that expense is coming out of *your* pocket, not theirs. The trillions of dollars globally in the sacrifices that literally are robbing human beings of lost productivity, food and raised standards of living are still not enough for Gaia's loyal followers. Man is simply a scourge to her well-being that must be diminished and removed in all possible ways-- except (of course) them because they are there to defend her and prevent her from being violated. They can stay and guard her "virginity" by offering as oblations and sacrifices the lives of those ruined by her subjects. Yeah, it's that silly.

139

# Second Amendment

Did you ever notice that every time there is a terrorist attack or a mass shooting the usual bunch of Democrats and liberals want to take your guns and restrict  more of your second amendment rights--as if taking away your guns would have prevented that attack? This can be traced back to illogical thinking on the part of the anti-gun lobby.

The Obama administration seemed at times hell-bent on doing whatever they could to curtail gun ownership in every way they could. They tried attacking lead as an EPA hazard (bullets are made with lead). They tried to sign on to international laws through the UN that would have implications to domestic gun laws. They even began using the free market by buying up the ammunition to the point that a $15 box of .22 caliber long bullets at one point sold for nearly $60 and 9mm ammo was often hard to find.

When it came to domestic terrorism, they failed to identify the real enemy (which is Islamic terrorism) and they had instead redirected their failures toward the NRA, Republicans, Christians, gun owners, veterans, etc. actually naming them as the greater threat to the nation. And because they were going after the wrong people, attacks by the mentally deranged and by radical Islamists multiplied during his administration. But there are always enough "useful idiots" out there that can be manipulated and will believe the narrative anyway. Doesn't it stand to reason that if the efforts they took to hunt down legal gun owners were instead directed at extinguishing ISIS that it would now be a dying loser (like Al Qaeda was late in George Bush's term) and that the westernized (American and English) Muslim punks would no longer be pledging allegiance to it? I wish these gun-grabbing Democrats would hate Islamic Terrorism as much as they hate law abiding American citizens. But they need to obfuscate the issue to deflect the rightful criticism they deserve.

Rights are inalienable and given from God. If they are granted by the government, then they can also be taken away. But life, liberty, and property--nobody can take away any of those without violating your inalienable rights. Implied in those rights are the amendments that we read in the Bill of Rights. The right to life, liberty, and property all imply the right to protect your life, liberty, and property. John Locke argued this in his treatises on government (two of them). His thinking influenced the nation's Founders and such ideas as "the consent of the governed" are direct quotes from his philosophy.

Legal here but a Crime There?

I believe that it's time for a national reciprocity law for concealed carry licenses. It's criminal that people can exercise their Second Amendment right to bear arms in most states freely, but will be arrested and jailed for five years for doing so in a few of the others. How can something so fundamental as your Second Amendment rights be treated so differently across the US? If it were the First Amendment (or any of the others) people would be furious at any curtailment of those rights. But, somehow, the Second Amendment is treated like a mistake by the Founders.

For those who may not know, the Second Amendment was placed right after the First because it was *that* important and because it is there to safeguard of all your other rights. When the Declaration of Independence stated that you have an inalienable "right to life, liberty and the pursuit of happiness" it implied in those rights are that you also have the right to protect yourself from those who would deny you those inalienable rights. That right to defend those rights was codified in the Second Amendment.

It's high time there is a full restoration of these rights to the people. Exercising your Constitutional right to bear arms should *never* be cause for your arrest, detainment or even harassment by law enforcement. Thank God it isn't in about forty-two states. But it's time that the law be applied evenly to every US citizen--including those in the other eight states.

You surrender your sovereignty and right of self-determination once you've made a deal with the devil. It was pointed out early in our Republic that the Brits don't have a Second Amendment and the implications of that was exactly what was argued by Madison in the Federalist Papers. It's worth quoting James Madison here in Federalist 46,

"Those who are best acquainted with the last successful resistance of this country against the British arms, will be most inclined to deny the possibility of it. Besides the advantage of being armed, which the Americans possess over the people of almost every other nation, the existence of subordinate governments, to which the people are attached, and by which the militia officers are appointed, forms a barrier against the enterprises of ambition, more insurmountable than any which a simple government of any form can admit of. Notwithstanding the military establishments in the several kingdoms of Europe, which are carried as far as the public resources will bear, the governments are afraid to trust the people with arms. And it is not certain, that with this aid alone they would not be able to shake off their yokes. But were the people to possess the additional advantages of local governments chosen by themselves, who could collect the national will and direct the national force, and of officers appointed out of the militia, by these governments, and attached both to them and to the militia, it may be affirmed with the greatest assurance, that the throne of every tyranny in Europe would be speedily overturned in spite of the legions which surround it."

Madison argued that the armed citizen was a check against a tyrannous government. He knew this firsthand having fought off the British during our own American revolution. I would never want to see that option exercised again because we've already seen what a Civil War can do to a country. About 615,000 Americans died to fight the last one in four short but deadly years from 1861-1865. But clearly that was partly why the Second Amendment was codified in our Bill or Rights.

I have a long time residence in New Jersey where I spent almost half the year. As I am sitting here, I am pondering the insanity and inequity of New Jersey gun laws which are also reflected in states like New York, Illinois, Massachusetts, etc. Having my primary residence in Florida, I have a license to carry a gun from that state. That license is recognized in the vast majority of the United States. But in New Jersey I am not allowed to carry my gun even though I am licensed. If someone were to pull a gun on me, I must beg for my life and possibly die. If a crime is being committed against me or my loved ones, I must cower and beg for mercy from the criminal. You have no right to life, nor the right to defend it here because New Jersey law makes everyone a victim of crime and makes it so *only* criminals have guns. What does it say about how New Jersey lawmakers look at the people they allegedly serve when they can't trust their own, law-abiding citizens to "keep and bear arms" as the Second Amendment states?

The politicians in New Jersey will say that the laws are meant to keep people safe. But just how effective are their laws to stop violence? Comparisons on this issue are easily made. New Jersey has a murder rate of 4.5 people per 100,000. Vermont has NO restriction on carrying guns (you don't even need a license) and their murder rate is 1.6 per 100,000. Yet even with some of the strictest gun laws in the nation, the city of Camden, NJ is still the number one murder capital in the USA. The places where the gun laws are the toughest are also where the murder rates are the highest. Think of Chicago. Think of Baltimore. Think of Washington DC. The little State of New Jersey has the distinction of being the only state with six cities in the top one hundred murder rates in the country: Atlantic City, Bridgeton, Camden, Newark, Patterson, and Trenton. Obviously our New Jersey state politicians *hate* liberty, *hate* the US Constitution and particularly hate the Second

Amendment. No matter how much lip-service they pay to liberty and civil rights, they are lying. This is a mental disorder which fails to let them grasp reality.


## Evil Exists

On Sunday, October 1, 2017 Stephen Paddock began shooting out of his hotel window at the Mandalay Casino killing at least 59 people and injuring 527 more. With victims lying in hospitals all around the city of Nevada, Democrats immediately began politicizing the event and calling for more gun laws—as if that will solve the problem of the evil of men's hearts. We've outlawed heroin, yet heroin is more available today than ever. We've outlawed machine guns, yet they are still available for purchase on the streets. In fact, short of going through the process of getting a Class III Federal Firearms license, the easiest way to get a machine gun is to find one on the streets in the black market. This is because criminals don't care how many laws we pass. You can ban all guns and you know who will still have them? Criminals. That's because the law abiding follow the laws. Criminals don't. I will state the obvious: Passing any more gun laws will only be "feel good" measures. They are like window dressing because they don't address the core issue. You can't pass laws to stop evil. Jeremiah in the Old Testament said it 2600 years ago, "The heart is deceitful above all things, and desperately wicked: who can know it?" (Jeremiah 17:9). It is people who kill people, guns are just tools to do it. So are bombs. So is anthrax. So are cars (as we've seen many times lately). So are chemicals. So are nukes. So are knives. Etc.

Stephen Paddock killed himself (as all cowards do) after his deed before the cops could get to him. But I don't think this guy had any mental sickness. He was extremely methodical. He planned this attack down to the details. He even had video cameras set up to see when someone was coming down the hallway where his room was. He had a cache of weapons. He had thousands of bullets. He had a suite that faced the venue he was targeting (a country music festival). He had the right type of guns to pull this off. This deed was very reasoned, methodical and planned to a hilt. So maybe you can call him a sociopath. But he did not have mental illness. He was very much a sane person and not much different than a guy like Timothy McVeigh. Had an agenda and carried it out.

We can say anyone who does this is mentally ill. But it becomes a matter of semantics. We have a hard time believing that this level of evil can exist in a person's heart. It scares us to think there are people who can be that heartless. But the fact that these people exist makes it more a reason why the good, law abiding people should be allowed to own guns.

Otherwise it will only be criminals who do. If there is a chance to stop someone from killing you or another human being, and you have the chance to do it, you should be able to. This will never end violence. But it levels the playing field.


Women's Rights?

The liberals here will say that women's lives matter—I guess except in New Jersey when they want to get a gun permit. Then they don't matter because God forbid one of those women wants to own a gun. They may end up protecting themselves and kill a crazy ex-boyfriend who has a knife. No, in *that* case, the murderous, knife wielding boyfriend needs to be protected against the possibility of an evil gun-toting woman.

Sadly, that is exactly what happened in the Spring of 2015 when Karen Bowne applied to get a gun in New Jersey knowing that her deranged ex-boyfriend, Michael Eitel, was violent and wanted to do her harm. Her restraining order against him didn't save her life when he came to her home and stabbed her with a knife. She had applied two months earlier for a gun permit which was still not approved. In most states you can walk into a gun store, show your drivers license, fill out the Firearms Transaction Record which is known as Form 4473 and the dealer does an

FBI uniform background check, and usually within a few days you can have your gun.

In my opinion, every time a murder or attempted murder is committed on someone who has tried to get a gun permit but either failed or was delayed by the bureaucracy, it should be seen as an act of malfeasance against the government that denied issuing it. The Second Amendment alone ought to be enough of a gun permit for people to acquire guns. There should be reasonable laws to prevent those unfit from owning them, but the burden of proof must lie on the state to show cause. The Second Amendment is a basic right and the presumption ought to always be that people have that right. Instead of citizens petitioning the government to exercise that right, it ought to only be taken away from those unfit (as they do with felons voting). We have it all backwards.

Power to the people.

I know that guns have been demonized by the left. There is a mentality out there that prevails among them that identifies a gun with malevolent intent. Having grown up in liberal New Jersey, I have seen that attitude and mentality firsthand. It is foolish, really, because the vast majority of gun owners are good, law abiding people. The vast majority of crimes involving a gun are done by those who have acquired them illegally, or because of past criminal records shouldn't even have a gun in the first place, and who almost certainly have never been trained in proper gun safety. It is almost a tautology to say that crimes involving guns are perpetrated by criminals, not by the law abiding. Seldom does a person go to the gun store to buy a gun legally and then go out and start killing people, robbing banks or do drive-by shootings with it. Yet this is how gun ownership is portrayed by some on the left. It is really just confusion and lies to mislead people for political purposes.

When a drunk driver kills someone with his car, we blame the driver. When a suicide bomber straps on a vest and blows up a marketplace filled with innocents, we blame the bomber. But somehow when a criminal kills people with a gun, liberals will find a way to blame guns. Can we do the same with cars next? Let's not forget that in 2016, in Nice, France, a Muslim jihadist killed 86 people and 458 were injured using a truck. I understand the logic they use when they say they want to address gun violence by stricter gun laws. But the logic is flawed.

151

# Prayer in School

I want to touch on a thought that has been on my mind for the past few years concerning the rapidly changing demographics of the USA. Some of you will disagree with me on this issue but I want you to hear me out before you do. As a former pastor for 16 years and a pastor emeritus after that till this day, I was always a man who wanted prayer back in school and Bible reading, etc. I believe that God's Word was the foundation upon which our country was built. The Bible gives context to many of the laws and much of the history of this nation. It is the reason that we place our hand on it and swear to tell the truth in a court of law. And I believe it was that same Word that helped to improve this nation by eventually getting rid of racism, giving women to right to vote, etc. because the Bible is clear on the equality of all people: "There is neither Jew nor Greek, there is neither bond nor free, there is neither male nor female: for ye are all one in Christ Jesus." (Galatians 3:28).

But what concerns me today is that these changing demographics are going to create a problem in the future--a problem which Christians may have faced already in their ministry of the Word. I have been asked to pray invocations, dedications, etc in several public settings. In my duties as a pastor, I opened the New Jersey legislative session in 1994 in prayer. I've dedicated several public buildings in southern New Jersey in prayer and have prayed at many Memorial Day parades, Independence Day gatherings, Veterans affairs, etc. You all know that *lately* these types of pubic events have often included a Rabbi and sometimes other religions--Hindu, Muslim, etc. I know that the truth will always prevail and will always set us free. And we know the One who is "the way the truth and the life" (John 14:6). But there may come a day that the public prayer may not even include a Christian. It may be hard to think of that now. But it is coming.

Some school systems already are closing for MUSLIM holidays. Atlantic City, NJ is one of them that I am aware of, but I bet there are others. I am not sure now that we want any "official prayer" in the public school because children who are not mature believers in Jesus may get confused and begin to take on a religious relativism the same way we are seeing moral relativism in society. Dare I say that the public school system has contributed greatly to that moral relativism. And do we really want an unbeliever teaching the Bible or leading in Bible reading *only* to afterwards ridicule what God's word says? I had a teacher once (back in the 1970's) who went through the Exodus story and pretty much tried to explain it all in non-miraculous terms. He tied the crossing of the Red Sea by the Jews in the Book of Exodus to the volcanic explosion of the Island of Santorni in the Mediterranean, saying the blood of the Nile River was red ash that spewed from the volcano before it blew, the changes in frogs and grasshopper migrations were also caused by this, etc. You get the idea. Let's be careful what we advocate!

The changes in US Demographics tell me that if we push for prayer in schools, or Bible reading, or religion in the public square, we may live to see the day (God forbid) that Islam gets a foothold in those places to the exclusion of Christianity. You already know that Christianity is readily mocked with impunity in just about every public venue. But Islam is not. The man who made that stupid movie that the Obama State Department blamed on the riots in the Middle East—including the deadly Benghazi attack in Libya--he was arrested and taken in for questioning because he insulted Islam! Is this still America? As much as it pains me to say this, the very things that we Christians have fought for (and I include myself in having fought for them, too) may be one day used against us to put religion in the public square---but instead of it being Christianity (as we may have envisioned) it will be Islam! Christians, I believe that we may need to take the stance that a secular state is best. That seems to be the wisdom of the Founding Fathers, though as you all know, many didn't hide their Christianity under the bushel.

These have been my thoughts of late. I don't believe that the Kingdom of God should be confused with politics. Paul told us "For our citizenship is in heaven; from which also we look for the Savior, the Lord Jesus Christ." (Philippians 3:20). History teaches us (the Catholic Church, the Church of England, the Middle Ages Muslim Califate, etc.) that letting religion and politics get too close to each other almost always bastardizes religion and seldom does any societal good.

I want to also point out again as a matter of background that I was raised as a Democrat and remained so until 1981 when I became born again and realized that the Democrat party was for abortion. Soon afterward I became a Republican and remained one for about 25 years until 2006, when I switched to independent because of the the inconsistencies in the party--and especially George Bush (who I voted for twice) regarding my faith. I now count myself a libertarian, but not a party Libertarian.

Now, if you disagree with me, you need to ask yourself what the alternative would be. You can say that laws can be passed to make Bible study mandatory in the context of US history. But then you are left with the issue of something that Christians hold dear—the Scriptures—being taught by people who may ridicule them. Similarly, if a moment of prayer is mandated in schools in the morning (for example), that prayer may be spoken by someone who is not even a believer. Does God hear such a prayer? Are we advocating dead traditions over a living relationship with God through Jesus? I can't see how the force of law can be seen in any way as beneficial to our cause. And how long before some Muslim sues and gets their prayers read over the school intercom in the morning? Then the Hindu. Then the Buddhist. Maybe eventually a Satanist.

This is why we need to be careful about what we ask.

# Monetary Policy

One of the questions that people never ask but they need to is: Are prices going up or is money going down? Does that sound confusing? It shouldn't be.  But I believe that it is the real issue and the reason it is not asked is because it reveals the underlying strategy that has been able to confiscate your money without you knowing it is happening.

The US government, by way of the Federal Reserve Bank, is in large part the blame for the cost of goods rising and the unaffordability of living in this country. Most people think that the price of goods--food, housing, gasoline, insurance, etc--just keeps rising as the natural course of the economy. But that is false and is actually a relatively recent phenomenon. The government is devaluing the currency and has been doing so since 1933. This, above most other causes, has been the real reason for inflation in this country. A study in the prices of most things prior to 1933 shows this to be true —especially relative to the time frame since then.

During the rise of the price of gold around 2008 and following, many people asked me why I didn't think gold was a good investment and how I have been wrong about it for awhile by then. It is true that when gold got to over $800 per ounce at that time I started being skeptical about its price and by the time it hit

$1000 per ounce I was convinced that it was over done. By the time this run was over it had hit over $1900 per ounce and I took what little gold I owned (just a few ounces), and I went and cashed them in at near those highs. It has since come down into the mid-$1200 per ounce range (where it stands as of this writing) and I am convinced that it is still high. So why am I so skeptical?

In order to understand the *value* of something verses the *price* of something I want to use an illustration. Say you are at a store and you wanted to buy a can of soda. If you paid $1.00 for that can, that would be its price. But if you are a smart shopper you also know that if you bought a six pack at the grocery store, it would be $2.99. So, is the value of that soda .50 or is it $1.00? What if you go to the County Fair and you get thirsty. The cans of soda there may be selling for $2.00 a can, or maybe at the movie theater they may be selling for $3.00. So, what's the value of that soda? Well, you know in your heart that it's only about 50 cents or so, but you are willing to pay $3.00 because you're thirsty. Your motivation for buying that inflated soda is *thirst not value.*

Now when gold was being priced at $1900 per ounce and people were paying it, why was that? The answer is really quite simple. They are being motivated by *fear*, and maybe also by some *greed*, believing two things: First, that gold will keep going up because the world is crumbling, and second, that we will all end up holding worthless dollar bills. I think people really knew in their hearts that gold is over-priced. But people also fear being left out and we are also a little greedy, thinking we can become trillionaires if we buy enough gold.

Valuation

So how do we properly value gold? Sometimes you need to use an unemotional proxy to determine the real value of something. One pretty good proxy that I think does well is real estate, which is a better measure of gold's value because it *tends* to remain relatively stable over long periods of time. Don't misunderstand me. Yes, home prices go up and they go down in value (mostly up). But those bumps and jags smooth out over the long term. So an illustration of valuation would help here.

Around 1910 my mom's house was built up in central New Jersey. Back at that time, it cost around $4500 have built. The person who had it built could have gone to the builder and paid him 450 of our US $10 gold pieces and that would have paid for it. At that time the usual way to make cash payments would have been in gold or silver. Those 450 gold $10 pieces represent about 225 oz of gold. In 1950, that gold would have been worth about $8600, and so was that house (give or take). In 1985 (after the last gold bubble popped) that gold would have been worth about $71,000, and the house about the same. In 2006, the house would have sold for over $375,000 but the gold was worth only $135,000. What happened? The HOUSE went DOWN to meet gold. In fact, a few years later the house and the price of gold were again in parity (about $250,000).

Today, the price of that gold is $275,000 and the house would still be worth about the same. So, eventually when gold is too high or the house price is too low, they will adjust over time. Chances are it will be gold will be the one that will move too high since it trades easier than homes, and a house will be more fairly valued in normal markets over the long haul.

So then, generally speaking over time, those 225 oz of gold would have been able to buy that same house through all the last 100+ years. When they couldn't, the house eventually came down, as in when the recent housing bubble crashed in 2006-07. At one point that gold could buy practically two of those houses. It needed to come down to meet the value of the home, or the home needed to rise to meet the gold, or a little of both (which is what happened). Mark my words. That is how values work over the long haul.

The only way that gold can remain high and never correct is if the world's economy collapses and a whole new paradigm is established. In that case, dollars will have no value and probably gold won't either. It will be about food and shelter at that point.

So, applying this lesson, let's thing about what has happened to our money. Think about this logically. A gallon of gasoline in 1962 when I was born was around 25¢. As of the writing of this book it is around $2.50 (depending where you live). But that same 1962 silver quarter that bought that gallon of gasoline in 1962 will still buy that gallon of gas today and give you almost $1.00 change! So, what happened? Did gas go up or did money go down?

Most people are not versed in monetary policy and economics to understand this, so they blame greedy corporations, or Saudi Arabia, or Exxon, or whatever. The *real* blame belongs to the government which can't stop spending money and is stealing value from your wallet every time they do. What I illustrated with gasoline is true of *everything* you buy, whether it is food, clothing, shelter, goods, supplies, transportation, etc.

The historical inflation rate from the inception of the USA in 1776 when we signed our Declaration of Independence till 1933 when we were taken off the gold standard by Franklin Roosevelt was negligible. There were some blips along the way (like during the Civil War), but for the most part most prices stayed mostly flat. But since 1933 a US dollar has lost about 95% of its value.

The process of these *thefts* started in in 1913 when the Federal Reserve system was established by Woodrow Wilson. But for the first twenty years they played by the same rules as the first 130 years of the nation. Then, in 1933, Roosevelt had the perfect opportunity to change things because of the Great Depression. He decided to try the Keynsian monetary experiment. He built fort Knox, demanded that all gold currency be turned in, and immediately devalued an ounce of gold from the long-standing established price about $20.00 to about $33.00--effectively allowing the printing of 50% more money overnight. By virtue of Bretton Woods agreement made ten years later, the US dollar was still pegged to gold--at least until Nixon finally took us off of it and allowed the dollar to float.

There is much more to monetary policy, but this is the basic idea that affects your wallet. Most people just buy the hype and don't place the blame where it belongs--a massive government that keeps growing by deficits. This, more than anything else, is stealing purchasing power from your money.

As Christians, we need to stand against the theft of working people's labor. The game that is being played is very subtle and few people will understand it. But what is happening is theft—plains and simple.

Things you should know

It is important for people to understand how the money game is played by the elite money movers. Think about this: Why does it seem when they agree to print more money that the stock markets seem to like it? The answer is actually quite simple: the less money is worth, the more money it takes to buy something-- even a stock. When the Federal Reserve decides to debauch the currency, it causes the stock market to adjust upwards to match the value of the company to the new lower value of the currency. That is why commodities also tend to rise on this news. It takes more dollars to buy a barrel of oil, an ounce of gold or even a share of stock.

I started asking this question back in 2011 when the national debt was about $14 trillion. Now it is almost $20 trillion and the stock market as of June of 2017 is at record highs. Who knows how much higher it can get? Much of the gain in the market the past eight years has been due to monetary policy. I know that at some point down the road this will cause another market collapse. It always does.

And, conversely, you will notice that when the Federal Reserve bank announces the possibility of a rate hike, the stock market goes down. This has been very troubling to market watchers because it is killing the working class and the people who save money—retirees and people who depend on savings. Never before has the federal government so openly promoted the wealth transfer away from the poor and middle class and to the very wealthy like this. To nearly double the national debt from 2009 to 2017 has also helped to nearly quadruple the US stock market, thus transferring much of that wealth to the super rich.  The S&P 500 hit a low of 666 (strangely) in the spring of 2009. As of the writing of this book in June of 2017 it is above 2400!

It is the St. Louis Federal Reserve Bank which is usually tasked to provides economic research charts and data through a bureau called FRED (i.e., federal reserve economic data). The chart that tells the big story in all of this is called EXCSRESNS, which is a measure of excess cash reserves being held by the bankers. Think about that for a moment. The chart below depicts *excess reserves* at the banks--not the required reserves for lending—which was at $2.2 trillion by March 2017. A look at this chart tells you that much of the newly printed money from federal government deficit spending is going to enrich the banks' balance sheets. (Incidentally, during the 2016 presidential election Hillary Clinton wanted to continue this policy and the bankers loved her so much that they were funding a big part of her presidential campaign!)

The law that governs this is part of the "too big to fail" strategy, the Dodd-Frank bill, and the Fed's ZIRP policy (i.e. zero interest rate policy) which made it more profitable to make money through a zero risk arbitrage than by making loans.

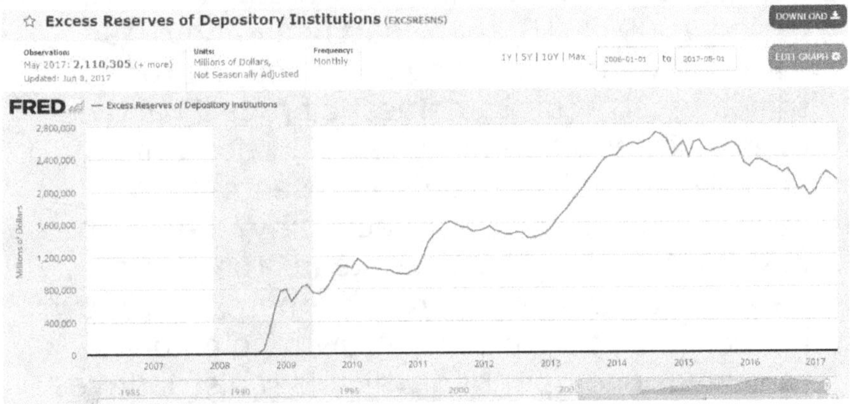


Now think about that. Banks are stashing money on their books rather than loaning it out for homes, cars, businesses, etc. to get the economy moving because they can simply hold government bonds and get paid without fear of foreclosures, repossessions, defaults, etc. They are getting money at near zero interest, buying 10 year bonds which are paying them between 1.5 and 2.5% interest, and have no risk. They just sit there and collect the interest payments.

This is why a rising stock market doesn't *always* indicate the growth of an economy. Sometimes it indicates growth of money supply--as in this case. During the decade of the 2010's, we've had an economy growing at a nominal 2%, but the deficits have added about 7% to GDP. What this means (in effect) is that we've had -5% REAL growth which has been masked by the 7% being added through government deficit spending.

Looking at the totals is even worse. From the period 2009-2016, there had been about $9 trillion in deficit spending and about $116 trillion in GDP (gross domestic product) activity over that period. That added debt accounts for about 7% of it. So if GDP represents the available pie in the entire economy, there is no new pie being made. That means there is no new wealth creation going on--there is NO new pie being made. The only growth going on is through money printing which is redistributive of wealth. That means that in a very real sense the pie is getting smaller and being cut into smaller slices to feed more people. It's like being asked "Do you want your pizza cut into 8 or 12 slices? and you answer 8 because you could never eat 12." The redistribution of wealth by currency devaluations is favoring the wealthiest.

Economist John Meynard Keynes once wrote in his book "The Economic Consequences of the Peace" that "Lenin was certainly right, there is no more positive, or subtle or surer means of destroying the existing basis of society than to debauch the currency. By a continuing process of inflation, governments can confiscate, secretly and unobserved, an important part of the wealth of the citizens. The process engages all of the hidden forces of economics on the side of destruction, and does it in a manner that not one man in a million can diagnose."

Adam Smith also decried the abuse of monetary policy when governments basically stole from the people to fund themselves. He writes, "I believe, the avarice and injustice of princes and sovereign states, abusing the confidence of their subjects, have by degrees diminished the real quantity of metal, which had been originally contained in their coins. The Roman as, in the latter ages of the republic, was reduced to the twenty-fourth part of its original value, and, instead of weighing a pound, came to weigh only half an ounce. The English pound and penny contain at present about a third only; the Scots pound and penny about a thirty-sixth; and the French pound and penny about a sixty-sixth part of their original value. By means of those operations, the princes and sovereign states which performed them were enabled, in appearance, to pay their debts and fulfil their engagements with a smaller quantity of silver than would otherwise have been requisite. It was indeed in appearance only; for their creditors were really defrauded of a part of what was due to them" (An Inquiry Into the Nature and Causes of the Wealth of Nations, Adam Smith, Chapter IV. Of the Origin and Use of Money).

I will list some specific numbers just so you can see it for yourself:

The 2016 GDP growth was at 2.9% and the deficit was at $587 billion which is near 3% of GDP. So that means basically that the growth in GDP that year was completely funded by newly printed money.

In 2015 the deficit was $439 billion, which is about 2.4% of GDP and the growth of GDP that year was also 2.4%. That means we had zero growth that year because all growth was borrowed/newly printed money. In 2015 the total nominal GDP for the USA was just under $18 trillion.

The total 2014 GDP was $17,348 billion and the total 2014 deficit was $483 billion of that money. The growth that years was listed at 2.4%, but the deficit represents about 2.8% of GDP. So, if 2.8% of the GDP was deficit spending and nominal growth was 2.4%, did the economy grow? Or, did it *shrink* by 0.4%?

In 2013 the federal government took in $680 billion less revenue than it spent (deficit), or about 4.1 percent of gross domestic product. But GDP *growth* was listed as 2.3%. So is that really growth, or actually a shrinkage of 1.8%?

In 2012, the deficit was $1.087 trillion which is 6.8 percent of GDP. But GDP *growth* was 2.1%. Or, did it actually shrink 4.7%?

In 2011 GDP *growth* was 1.6%, the deficit was $1.3 trillion which was equal to 8.6% of GDP. So the economy actually *shrank* 7% in 2011.

In 2010 GDP *growth* was 2.5%, but the deficit was 1.294 trillion which was 8.7% of GDP. That means the economy effectively shrank 6.2%.

Do you understand the cruel joke yet? The Obama administration had overseen about 22% in cumulative shrinkage of the US economy which was masked by over $9 trillion in national debt. And everyone feels it to this day. The middle class is making about the same money that they did 20 years ago (inflation adjusted). There are less jobs, less people in the workforce, more people collecting government checks. Look around you. The factories, the mills, the mines, the manufacturers--they are all closed. Even many stores are empty.

The sad truth is that you are being fed 100% lies my friends, and most people are buying it because either they don't understand the economics behind it or they don't want to understand economics. Anytime that the federal government prints money (i.e., issues debt via treasuries and bonds) to spend in deficit, that is not creating economic growth, it is masking economic decline by expanding the debt.

Think about it on a personal level. If you keep buying stuff with a credit card, your neighbors might think you're rich--nice house, nice cloths, nice car, vacations, etc. But your accountant will tell you differently. That is exactly what the government has done. This is a debt driven bubble. They are paying the bills with credit cards. The only ones making money are the one's who want to keep this charade going--the elite, the banksters, paper pushers, rule makers, money shufflers, etc. They don't produce anything, but they make billions by skimming your sweat and keeping a portion. If they all disappeared today you would never miss them. Yet, they are the ultra-wealthy. These are backers of establishment class, political class politicians! These are the one's who funded Hillary Clinton's 2016 presidential campaign and Barack Obama's 2008 campaign! They are also the ones who funded BOTH Obama's and Romney's 2012 campaign. It really didn't matter who was elected because they saw the game continuing. It is also why they hate Trump so much. He doesn't care about them.


Audit the Federal Reserve Bank.

This issue is bigger than many people think. The Federal Reserve Bank has been printing money in order to meet our government's spending spree for almost 100 years now. Every time the Federal Government wants to spend money, it can only get that money from two sources: It can either get it from taxes or it can get it from borrowing. When the government gets it from taxes, it is a straightforward process. You send it in and they spend it. But when they get the money from borrowing, it is a different story.

The Treasury issues bonds which are guaranteed by the government. A bond is simply a loan from whoever buys it. When you buy $100 in bonds from the government, you are lending them money and they are paying you back interest. Depending on the interest rates, that bond will get varied rate of return. The biggest buyers of bonds are the banks. The Federal Reserve is not supposed to buy them directly, but indirectly through a bank. This is because it would be too easy for the Treasury to simply print up the bonds and have the Federal Reserve buy them with freshly printed money. There would be no constraints and the value of dollar would be unchecked. So, to make sure there is *real* demand for those bonds, the Treasury sells them to banks, individuals, other countries (China, Japan, etc.), trusts, mutual funds, hedge funds, etc.

Now, the Federal Reserve will buy them from other banks when it wants to add newly printed money into the system. This way the money is based on a real asset, not just on imaginary paper. The problem is that this system is based on debt. In other words, every dollar that enters into circulation is through debt that comes from bonds. There is no real backing to that money. It is not gold or silver. It is paper that was printed in order to buy bonds. The expansion of money supply automatically means that there are more dollars chasing after the same amount of goods. "Economic growth" is skewed by the entrance of this kind of money into the system. In a sense, it is not all growth. Some of it is monetary expansion. We are being duped by those who count money and are keeping score.

When you think about inflation, you need to think about it the right way. It isn't that greedy people are raising prices. It is that the government is making your money worth less. They have been devalued by the Federal Reserve's policy of printing money.

In 1933 when Franklin D Roosevelt took us off the gold standard, every dollar was backed by silver or gold. Your money was *really* worth something. Today, your money is faith-based. It has no real worth. It is built on promises. We don't even have a real grasp of how much money is out there--real, printed money and money that is on balance sheets or IOUs. This means that theoretically one day your money can become worthless. It has happened in the past. It can happen again.

For this reason, I believe that it is time to audit the Federal Reserve's books. Let the American people know what is really going on with their money. Since money represents your entire life--your home, your cars, your labor, your retirements, everything you own--it is necessary that we know what it is really worth. Otherwise, we may find one day that we are selling our home for a stack of worthless paper. Think of it another way: You are selling your life one hour at a time to your employer. Money represents increments of you very life, your time on earth. What is *that* worth?

I think it is time that we wake up America. If you love your kids, you will vote out of office any and all so-called "progressives", liberals, just about all Democrats, and a good percentage of Republicans. The real difference today between the Republican Party and Democrat Party is Big Government vs. Bigger Government. Both parties have been complicit in stealing your kids' future.

What Makes the Poor, Poorer?

Looking at this a little differently, on March 1, 1956 minimum wage was changed to $1.00/hr. Taking the value of $1.00 of 1956 currency (quarters, dimes or halves made of silver), you get $12.65 in today's value. But federal minimum wage right now is $7.25, which is

$5.40 or about 43% less in purchasing power. So minimum wage has not kept up with currency devaluation. But that year (1956) government represented about 23% of total GDP and today that number stands at over 35%, an increase of about 50%. In order to fund that increase in share of GDP spending, something had to give. The most nondescript way for politicians and bureaucrats to increase their share of GDP for their ambitions and projects without raising the ire of the citizens is the backdoor approach of currency devaluation. This way the blame can be placed on greedy corporations raising their prices and a narrative of class envy can ensue. Diabolical and sinister are two words that come to mind.

Now, it is invalid to say that the minimum wage laws should be changed to reflect inflation because it is the government--not industry—that has taken the working class' share of GDP. In fact, industry has greatly diminished as a percentage of GDP over that same time frame. And yet, they are the real wealth and job creators. Government doesn't create wealth.  It is dependent on those who do create wealth to subsist off them.

It is obvious that factories, plants, mills, mines, etc. have been closing down never to reopen. Again, just look around you. But government just takes from industry and from laborers to redistribute it at will—over half of it in various entitlement programs which help to further fuel unemployment. So, it is the government that has encroached on the private sector's share of GDP and has done so primarily through the "money games" of monetary policy.  At some point the private sector will no longer be able to support the public sector and entitlements. Then what? An economic collapse and social unrest will certainly follow. This is not doomsday prophesying. This is a hard look at reality.

To be sure, some corporations have grossly abused their people. They have cut jobs in the US and replaced them with jobs overseas. Some CEOs get paid obscene salaries and have plundered the companies they run. But, for the most part, they are the exception and not the rule. It isn't some malevolent scheme to hurt the working class regardless of how often you hear liberals screaming about it. In fact, liberalism favors government getting even *more* involved--meaning that they will end up taking an even greater share of GDP!

The calculations corporations use to make decisions on jobs, expansion, factory openings and closings, etc. are strictly based on economics. And the US government has created a hostile economic environment to most industry. That is the real bottom line. It is more economical to mine coal and iron ore in Pennsylvania or Kentucky, put it on trains to California, send it to China on ships, have them smelt it using our coal and fabricate it into parts with cheap labor, then send the fabricated parts back to the US, than it is to do it here using our laborers and our factories. Our laws, rules, regulations, policies have made it that way. Don't blame cheap Chinese labor alone. That is only a part of the equation.

If the US is going to get back to a thriving economy, it will need to have major changes in policy. We will need to stop devaluing currency so that government can expand its reaches into every facet of life. We will need to curtail its size and scope, returning to the Constitutional authority of its enumerated powers, and no more. We will have to incentivize industry to hire and expand by providing favorable regulatory environment, tax treatment, and a truly free market devoid of government obstructionism.

Let the businesses that are economically viable succeed and let those that aren't fail. Let the marketplace determine price. Remove monopolies and protectionism. Allow supply and demand to reign BOTH in purchasing AND in labor markets. People want to work. But work has been disincentivized by robust entitlement programs. Business has been disincentivized by over-regulation and heavy taxation.

In the transition from the crony capitalist system we have now to the free market system we should move to, let there be favorable treatment for those industries that hire workers. Let there be favorable treatment to those that raise pay. Let there be favorable treatment to those that contribute to society's good. Remove all lobbying and let government contracts be done by lowest bid, common sense substitution, accepted or rejected by unbiased citizen panels from across the country and spectrum of people.

These things (and lots more) can be done to turn this country around and reinvigorate our economy. I hope congress will wake up and realize that they've been an obstruction to revitalizing the American economy. Get out of the way and let entrepreneurs do their thing. The poor will thrive when they have jobs and can choose the ones that pay them best and treat them best. And they will thrive when the government stops stealing a portion of their labors through monetary games.

# Xenophiles

For the sake of my family's safety, I oppose the indiscriminate entry of foreigners into the USA. Those of a more liberal persuasion believe it is the right thing to do. But let's get something straight: As a Christian I believe we ought to help anyone who crosses our path that has a genuine need. That includes the Syrian people who were being displaced by the war in their country. But to somehow associate that with letting them come to the USA is a false choice. The world community has the power to stop this in its tracks and yet they have instead made the suffering refugees into a political issue and a part of their globalist agenda.

From the standpoint of genuine compassion, ask yourself if any one of you would prefer to stay in the land you love, the country that speaks your language, the place your family lives *or* to uproot and leave to a foreign land that has no connection to you or your lifestyle? Real compassion would be for world leaders to get off their collective derrieres and take action--military, security, compassionate, etc. Set up refugee safe zones and give them the aid they need. And if you "love your neighbor as yourself" you will protect him and do whatever you can to fight those who would perpetrate evil upon him. But it really isn't about that.

Instead we have politicians using the suffering masses as pawns in their overall destabilization strategies to edge us closer to their globalist goals. I am especially concerned that Christians are being dragged into this through the exploitation of our religious beliefs by those who are just as willing to jail you for protesting abortion or not wanting to participate in a gay ceremony or who want to shut you up when you speak about Jesus. They will invoke Christian words and ideas much like Hitler did in Nazi Germany only to make their point while having no real loyalty to the truth or to Christ. Don't be fooled by this manipulation of your faith. They are using you.

Besides, there are many who basically argue that we should have open borders. But what is a nation without borders? What does it mean to be a citizen in that situation? If we simply occupy space and do not give back to the place we live, how are the commons maintained? The roads, schools, military, and all of the infrastructure that we all enjoy needs money to build and maintain it.

When the liberals say that this is a moral issue, remember that there are two moral sides to this argument. Saying that illegals are humans, too, and need our help is only one side of it. But the working class citizens who have invested their blood, sweat, tears, heart and soul into a community also have a moral side. How is it fair for them to pay for everyone? Isn't that also immoral? The financial struggles of the US taxpaying citizen is seldom accounted for in these arguments.

This is why the argument is false compassion. This is an argument made by carefully nuanced selective facts made to appear like a compassionate argument, but really it just amounts to nothing more than manipulative propaganda. There is no honesty in this debate, just an agenda to allow the nation to swell in numbers of illegals with the greater goal of corralling them into a political voting block. You've heard Democrat strategists say it often: That the demographic trend of more Hispanics favors our strategy. And that reveals their real goal which masquerades as compassion.

Furthermore, I think that the US needs to stop all foreign aid. No, this doesn't contradict what I just said about helping refugees. Actually, I think this is a no brainer.

Let me make two points here. First, most of the nations that get our aid have no care what is in the best interest of the USA. They are happy to take whatever American money they can get and will ask for more.  They will treat us like friends, but will quickly stab us in the back. Just look at how many of them vote against us in the United Nations and that fact is easily ascertained. It is the politically expedient thing to do in foreign nations. Talk against the Americans and you will gain friends.

The second point is even more profound. It is a fact that much of our aid never gets to the poor. We often pay people who hate us and work against us. Why pay them when they can hate us for free? When you visit the capital cities of many of the nations that receive American aid, what you see is ambassadorial mansions surrounded by paved driveways with a Rolls Royce and elaborate water fountains. This, while a few blocks away their people are eating mud pies and dying of cholera. Where is the aid going? The mansion tells a story that their empty words could never tell. The American public is told that we give foreign aid to the desperately poor people of some given nation, and are shown pictures of unwashed children with protruding bellies and flies buzzing around their faces, as if those are the kids getting the aid. But they aren't. When those kids DO get aid, it is usually from Christian missions organizations doing the work and almost never the United Nations.

As for "humanitarian aid", I believe that the US is the most generous country on earth--and statistics on our charitable donations prove it. So, the most efficient and sure way for help to get there is to let private charities take care of any humanitarian needs that exist out there. The Red Cross, Salvation Army, various missionary organizations, Doctors Without

Borders, etc. They are far more effective than governments and the money doesn't end up buying palaces and high end cars for diplomats and dictators.

As far as foreign military aid (which is a bigger chuck of so-called "foreign aid"), all that is doing is funding the "Military Industrial Complex" that Dwight Eisenhower spoke of in his famous farewell speech by the sweat of the American taxpayer. It also often puts us in wars we shouldn't be in because, along with those war machines we sell comes advisers to show them how to use it. Mission creep is a very real thing and we need to avoid it at all costs. It ends up being our sons and daughters who will fight the next conflict. Besides, do we really want to pay higher taxes to send our money to nations for a war that has nothing to do with us?

I *fully* understand the reasoning behind our entry to Korea, Vietnam, Gulf War, etc. But the reasoning was flawed. Which of you would give up their son or daughter's life to fight for Korea? Vietnam? Iraq? We have used a false sense of "nationalism" to morally justify our entrance into those wars. And there were many empty seats at Thanksgiving last year all across the United States because of those wars. And those seats won't be filled this year either. Those sons and daughters died as heroes in the service of our country. But in many cases our country was doing the wrong thing. Their patriotism isn't in question, but the wisdom of our leaders certainly is.

Our government can also regulate to whom we sell arms. We don't have to sell to those we think may be a threat to peace, or who abuse human rights, etc. We can sell arms to Israel, for example, to defend itself against just about all of its Muslim neighbors. They don't need us to simply *give* them the arms. They have a thriving capitalist economy and they have compulsory military service for all citizens. Our "military aid" comes with too many strings for them, anyway--as we have seen recently with their "Iranian problem." We need to let them exercise their sovereign, God-given right to defend themselves without the USA telling them when, where, and if they can.

I am not saying that we should completely shut off any immigration, or turn our back to any genuine need in the world. But I am saying that immigration policy should favor the United States and immigrants should be entering bringing skills and enriching the nation unless they are allowed in as specific types of refugees. And I am also saying that our humanitarian aid needs to be done through known, vetted private charities who are held accountable rather than by the untrustworthy thieves at the United Nations.

# Islamophobes

"I have come here to seek a new beginning between the United States and Muslims around the world; one based upon mutual interest and mutual respect; and one based upon the truth that America and Islam are not exclusive, and need not be in competition. Instead, they overlap, and share common principles - principles of justice and progress; tolerance and the dignity of all human beings... throughout history, Islam has demonstrated through words and deeds the possibilities of religious tolerance and racial equality."
~~~~~President Barack Obama, Cairo Egypt, June 4, 2009

One of the repeated themes you hear in all of the Islamic terrorism stories is how the perpetrator was just a normal, run of the mill guy who was fun-loving and a decent person. Then they become "religious" and often go on some pilgrimage to Pakistan, Afghanistan, Saudi Arabia, etc. and come back to commit these acts. In some cases just the mere fact that they became more "religious" does it and there is no associated pilgrimage.

If the critical mind cannot connect the dots and conclude that radicalization is something endemic to Islam itself, then we will *never* fix this problem. Let me say it very clearly, unequivocally and unambiguously:
~~~~~

*Fundamental Islam breeds terrorism*. The Q'ran, among many other things, is also a book of terrorism. I hear that moderate Muslims disprove that thesis. But so-called "moderate Muslims" are really people who have the religious traditions and even the culture of Islam without taking the teachings to their conclusion. The ones we call "radical Muslims" are ones who follow the Q'ran and the various Hadith faithfully, wanting to live out the teachings in their lives. The story of almost every Islamic bomber, murderer, terrorist that has struck on our US soil follows the same theme of radicalization. When you hear that some Muslim became "more religious," I say *look out*!

It may not be politically correct to say so, but Islam is not only a religion. It is also a very comprehensive world view and a way of life that includes laws, punishment, culture, society, food, family, education and government. It is not only a religion. We can't simply associate Islam in our minds to Christianity or Judaism and believe that it is a religion that deserves similar protection. It is more analogous to Nazism or Communism than to Judaism or Christianity. Until we understand this, we will continue to fail in this war against terror.

It's Islam that has a problem. It's not us. A central part of Islam is a worldview that has as its ultimate goal global domination, subjugation of unbelievers, a society based on sharia law, devoid of the western ideals of human rights as we all understand them. Gays will be put to death; women will be kept silent, subjugated, and completely veiled; speech will not be free; Islam will be the only religion openly tolerated; the use of any intoxicants will lead to severe punishment or death; the deflowering of little children is acceptable, etc. This is not xenophobia or Islamophobia. This is a statement of facts. Only someone that is completely *stupid* and willfully *blind* will not acknowledge this. Meanwhile, the attacks on the west keep mounting.

Why did we have attacks against New York City? Why Paris? Why Boston? Why San Bernardino? Why Chattanooga? Why Ft. Hood? Why Brussels? Why Orlando? Why Manchester?

One of the things that we in the west have to face is that Islam doesn't value the individual like we do. The western tradition within Judaism and Christianity is that "man is created in the image of God" and that, as such, he holds a unique place in the world which is higher than the animals and all of nature. For this reason, the act of murder was once considered as act of blasphemy against the image of God. This is the thinking gave rise to the wording in the Declaration of Independence and to the Bill of Rights.

Regardless of the lip service you hear from some, Islam's values are different. All you need to know is demonstrated by their acts of suicide bombing, use of human shields to protect arsenals, placing of weaponry in schools and hospitals, and the targeting of civilians and non-belligerents--not only by terrorists, but even by sovereign states like Iran, Iraq, Syria, Afghanistan, and yes even Turkey.

This major difference in values also works against us. To threaten them with retribution is laughable in their eyes. They invite it. They put bombs on their children and gladly give them up to death. There are numerous Youtube videos that even show "glad mothers" interviewed by Israeli journalists about the joy of knowing their son blew himself up for the cause of Allah. One mother said "Now is my life fulfilled. Now is my joy complete. Now have I found real happiness" after her son killed himself and several Israelis in a jihadist attack. I suspect that any humanity that is left inside a mother like that is actually crying inside, but a blind stoicism is what her culture expects and she is glad to deliver it, albeit with pain. This is not the enemy that we are used to fighting in the past. Allowing them to enter our country freely is to be ignorant of these differences.

Not all Muslims are going to teach their kids to kill. But how many times have you heard by now that the parents of bombers, suicide killers, mass shooters, etc are "shocked" at what their kids did? Shocked? Why would they be shocked? Wake up! It's Islam. Islam is easily subject to violence because the Q'ran and the various hadith teaches it. The parents usually escaped their Islamic country with the ideals of western life in mind. They came here embracing the idea of a more liberalized life. But their children often didn't make that decision and as they explore their own roots, their own identity as Muslims in a foreign land, they can easily become radicalized—and they often do.

While the servants of Allah believed they were doing the will of Allah as Mohamed expressed it in the Q'ran, the servants of the Lord Jesus Christ were doing His will as expressed in the New Testament. Which one do you think is God? And which one is Satan himself? It is as clear as it can be. Jesus said it best, "Ye shall know them by their fruits." If you are a liberal and think what I am saying is wrong, please keep your defense of Islam to yourself because I am quite honestly sick of hearing it and it not only wreaks of hypocrisy coming from alleged "liberal-minded people" but in a moment of candor I want to tell you further that it's a crock of lies. You can go tell it to the politically correct because I will have none of it. You can't confront a problem if you don't believe it exists.  Even many Muslims believe it exists, so why can't many liberals? Simply, because it goes against their multiculturalism doctrines.

Now, lest you get the wrong impression, there is a segment of Islam--just like in Christianity--that is simply nominal. A person who says he is a Christian, but who denies the Virgin Birth or the vicarious atonement is not a Christian, no matter how much he calls himself such. I don't care that he goes to church—possibly even every Sunday. A preacher once rightly quipped "If going to church makes you a Christian, then standing in a garage must make you a car." The truth is that some "Christians" are just nominal, meaning a Christian in name only. For a person to be a Christian he must believe the teachings found in the Bible because our faith comes from that book. The same holds true for Muslims. A true Muslim must believe the teachings of the Q'ran if he is to be considered a real Muslim. Islam and Christianity are belief systems, not matters of genetics or race.

A committed Muslim who follows the Q'ran will do what the Q'ran says. He will study the Hadith and want to know how it applies to his life. He will practice the teachings of Mohamed--just like any good Christian will practice Jesus' teachings. The literal teachings of the Q'ran are what terrorists follow. They are trying to implement a global caliphate. They divide the world into two parts: Believers in true Islam who will rule the world, or infidels who must convert or be subjugated and even die. There is no peaceful co-existence in the Q'ran. That is a fabrication as any believing

Muslim will tell you. This is why fundamentalist Muslims kill other Muslims who they view as compromisers of the faith. To them, they have denied the faith and, having known better because they claim Islam, they must die for their infidelity.

Some people may not see things so black and white and are of a more liberal persuasion. OK, but I will say this emphatically: Just as there are certain things Muslims must believe to be true Muslims, there are also certain things which must be held to in order to even be a Christian, by definition.

The mistake people make is to believe that Christianity is simply a matter of self-identification. Being a Christian only starts as self-identification. But Christianity is not whether you accept God on your terms, but whether God accepts you because you've come to Him on *His terms*. It's not your call, ultimately, what you can pick and choose to believe. This is not a metaphysical buffet where you pick what you like. He's God, you're not. Modern man—especially younger people like Millennials—have a hard time with this because it sounds absolutist. Well, it is. Jesus is the Lord and you are His servant. That word Lord in the New Testament is "κύριος" and it means "master."

Finally, there is a major difference in practice. A true Christian following the teachings of

Jesus in the Sermon on the Mount prays for his enemies, tries to win people who are unbelievers by telling of Jesus' love, and encourages nominal Christians to get serious and live out their faith. A true Muslims kills his enemies, converts or kills unbelievers, and kills Muslims who are nominal as a blasphemer and an infidel.

The root word on Islam or Muslim is the trilateral root *slm.* Though etymologically it has been tied to the Hebrew word *shalom,* it has morphed to mean *submission*. That is ultimately what Islam teaches, the submission of a person to Allah as he is revealed in the Q'ran. As a matter of theology, I can't argue with this thought. It is what Christianity also teaches. But Allah is not the God of the Bible. And the teachings of Mohamed are not the teachings of Jesus.

After the San Bernardino, CA massacre on December 2, 2015 where 14 people were killed and 22 more were injured, carried out by a married Muslim couple, Syed Rizwan Farook and Tashfeen Malik, there was a news report about the mother of Syed claiming absolute ignorance about his radicalization. At that point the thought crossed my mind that if the mother of that San Bernardino terrorist didn't know that her own son and daughter-in-law were radicals, doesn't that speak to the nature of Islam? Radicals often attend mosques which Muslims will swear are peaceful. So the difference between radical Islam and "peaceful Islam" must be so slim that they are essentially the same thing. And that makes sense because the Q'ran teaches violence in may ways. Islam itself has enough radical ideas that are part of the mainstream that the difference is unclear. The only difference I see is that a peaceful Muslim believes and harbors certain hate inwardly, while a radical one believes and acts on it.

I want to draw an analogy here. People who drink alcohol have the potential to become alcoholics. Not all who drink become alcoholics. In fact, most do not. But the correlations are so high that everyone knows the potential is there. Similarly, people who expose themselves to Islam and the Q'ran have the potential to become terrorists. Not all who are Muslims become terrorists. In fact, most do not. But the correlations are so high that everyone knows the potential is there.

It seems that we now are living in a non-scientific age where cause-and-effect has been subjugated to political correctness. There are terrorist acts every day around the globe racking up body counts into the thousands. Those who are dying are almost always innocents, not belligerents. But somehow the "progressive" segment of society refuses to make the correlation even though it is as obvious as the nose on their face.

Now, before you tell me about the KKK or Timothy McVeigh or the Crusades or the Catholic Inquisition, please realize that you are making several logical mistakes. First, you are being anachronistic. Nobody is dying today by the Crusades or the inquisition. And I haven't heard of the KKK doing many lynchings ever since Democrats abandoned them in the 1960s. This is a diversion and denial of present reality.

Secondly, you are arguing a genetic fallacy as to the question of "why." Islam teaches violence. Christianity doesn't. Christians and Muslims both have the ability to kill. But Islam teaches killing and Christianity teaches love. Muslims kill *for* Allah while Christians kill *despite* Jesus. Muslims kill believing their deeds are righteous. Christians kill knowing their deeds are sin. Anyone who reads the texts can see it clearly. Those who haven't studied the New Testament and the Q'ran, are ignorant in their opinions to make any moral equivalency of the two. Without having studied the New Testament, you may have the opinion that Christianity allows for killing your enemy. It doesn't. But the Q'ran does. Without having studied Islam you wouldn't know that.

Thirdly, you are arguing a categorical error as to the question of "who." It isn't Christians, who are numerous in this country--possibly 75% of it--who are potentially terrorists. It is Muslims who are just 1% of the population.

The bombings and murders going on are never done by the Presbyterian Women's Auxiliary or by Women Aglow. It's not the Salvation Army, Campus Crusade for Christ or the Navigators International. It's Muslims. When you turn on the TV and there has been a mass shooting or a bombing somewhere, you know in your heart before the announcement that yet another Muslim has expressed his faith in Allah. And almost every time you'd be correct in that assumption.

Lastly, you are arguing a false magnitude in this problem. Despite the fact that Christians may kill people, it is relatively rare. You can count them on one hand. There is no Christian terrorism epidemic. But Muslims kill every day around the world. We are talking specifically Islamic terrorism. And it is epidemic. To deny this is to stand in the camp with idiots. Christianity does not teach killing and those who do it cannot claim the teachings of Christ for their deeds. But there will always be that select few who do so anyway. It is not common, but it has happened.

If you don't like what I am saying, examine yourself. Admitting there is a problem is the first step to recovery. And our world needs recovery badly.

Furthermore, hiding this problem from an unsuspecting world is actually a part of the scheme. Islam has always had a problem with truthfulness. The Islamic practice of *taqiya* basically allows for Muslims to lie about anything—even Islam—if they perceive that it will advance their cause. This is a matter of Islamic doctrine. A good Muslim can make claims about many things which are patently false, yet they will look you in the eye and swear by Allah they are the truth. They do it without shame because they are permitted to. They will twist an account of some incident and even distort history to make their point.

In fact, it is no surprise that few Islamic universities study the antiquities and archaeology because the Q'ran is so wrong on history. They have made claims about history that are so bizarre and so easily disprovable that it is seldom you will see any department of antiquities in Muslim institutions of higher learning. They just simply aren't there. The Q'ran has made claims about the New Testament, about the Old Testament, about various historic events that archaeological discoveries have since clearly disproven. So it shouldn't surprise us (for example) that ISIS was ploughing under Assyrian Kingdom artifacts in Iraq since Assyria is mentioned many times in the Old Testament. They will tell you they are destroying idols. But it is actually historic revisionism in the making.

198

A Plea

This past spring as my family were getting ready to go to church and hear happy sermons about moms and Mothers Day, it struck me that in many parts of the world there are women who are being treated as chattel, being used as sexual slaves, being bought and sold for the purpose of being used and abused. This is being done in the name of their "god" (Allah) and under the cover and sanction of religious devotion. The disparate differences between that "religion" (Islam) and real Christianity couldn't be more pronounced, where women (and all people) are regarded as equals before God. It saddened me to know that these women will bear sons who will then turn against women--and, by extension, their own mothers, because, obviously, no son was ever born without a mother. This alone should stand as an apologetic against that so-called "god" and his followers--a "god" who is none other than the "god of this world" (II Corinthians 4:4).

# Israel

The Jewish success and Israel's success in history should not be a surprise to those who have read the Bible and understand history. God has stated in both the Old Testament and the New Testament that Israel has a special place in His heart and His plan. I think it is a mistake for Christians to dismiss that—despite the fact that some Christians have taught Israel is no longer relevant is God's plans. Perhaps they haven't read the Revelation.

With our presidents and diplomats always going to Israel on missions of peace and attempts to reconcile with the Palestinians I thought I would offer my thoughts on the Jews.  The question I want to ask is why have the Jews been generally so successful in a world that has often hated and persecuted them? In my opinion, there is a spiritual component and a utilitarian component to the answer. I have a few observations.

As a Christian it is no surprise that my Jewish friends have excelled in many areas. Spiritually, I believe they have the Abrahamic blessing from God upon them and that it is both conditional but also irrevocable. For example, as of the writing of this book in 2017, Nobel Prizes have been awarded to 881 individuals, of whom 197 (22.4%) were Jews. This is true, yet people of Jewish descent comprise less than 0.2% of the world's population. After 2000 years of exile, the nation of Israel was miraculously reconstituted in 1948. This is no accident. The little state of Israel which is no bigger than New Jersey is able to stand firm in a region of hostile neighbors. It defends itself and wins against bigger nations and poor odds. You may say it is because of the US. And, indeed, that is true. But the blessing the US has been to Israel has also been reciprocated to the US. We are also divinely blessed for being a friend to Israel. This is a mutual blessing and it is divine, not human. God has given them this blessing and unless you are well-versed in the Bible-- particularly in the Old Testament--you will simply gloss this over. But God told Abraham, "And I will bless them that bless thee, and curse him that curseth thee: and in thee shall all families of the earth be blessed" (Genesis 12:3). That is the spiritual basis of this all and it was given to the Father of the Jews, Abraham. It was subsequently passed on to Isaac and then Jacob, who is better known as Israel.

As a practical matter, Jews have had to fight to survive in an often antisemitic world. As a Christian, I must sadly confess that this antisemitism often came from various Christian sects who have misappropriated Bible verses to justify their hatred. It has also come from many Muslims who have taught Jew hatred as a matter of religious doctrine. But I believe that this survivalism has helped to push excellence, achievement, intelligence and nimbleness among Jews simply to overcome the hatred and persecution. Also, with a long chequered history of being forbidden to own land, or even to operate in the open, many times they had to find creative and innovative ways to make a living and survive. Is this an evolutionary mechanism in play? Perhaps so— at least in this case. Add to that a cultural and religious insistence on literacy (in order to read the Torah) and the deliberate inbreeding within their population (again, religiously motivated) and this serves to further keep their gene pool free of weakness that may be found in other populations. Higher IQ, innovation, creativity and industry are desirable survival traits when persecution, flight and resistance have been the way of life for nearly two millennia in exile.

It should never be a question whether Christians support the Jewish people and the state of Israel. As a matter of Biblical teaching we should and as a matter of Christian teaching, we ought to love them as those whom God has on His heart. Paul said it best when he wrote "As concerning the gospel, they [the Jews] are enemies for your sakes: but as touching the election, they are beloved for the fathers' sakes. For the gifts and calling of God are without repentance," Romans 11:28-29. That is, God loves them because they are descendants of Abraham, Isaac and Jacob.

I suspect that as long as the United States continues to be a friend to Israel and to the Jewish people, we will also continue to reap the spiritual benefit that God bestows upon those who demonstrate blessing to Abraham's descendants. But if this country ever turns its back on them, I fear the future. The Obama administration certainly came close to doing that. Who knows what political moves lie ahead concerning Israel? Our future leaders would do well to know this spiritual connection.

# Breakdown of Social Order

It is no surprise that our American society is breaking down. Respect for authority is failing because authority has often been found to be overreaching. This will affect teachers, cops, politicians, and most government entities in the future. A healthy respect for authority needs to be restored. But respect in the real world is earned. The US needs to back away from micro-managing people's lives and turning every citizen into a criminal. The ubiquity of government in your every day life needs to cease. We are creating a monster in society and a beast in government--and BOTH are getting ready to attack each other. This is *not* civil order! And to just strengthen the resolve to force civil order by toughening up laws, policing, fines, penalties--whatever--will only escalate this distrust and probably make things worse. Fundamentally, people want to be free and *only* those who violate the rights of others ought to face the law. That is how the law should work.

The issue that I think we need to face is how big, how intrusive, how deep into your wallet and life should government be allowed to go? In my opinion, that is the root of all of this civil discord. And, I know there will be some who won't be able to see the connection, but the government funding the war on poverty is probably the biggest culprit in society's breakdown. Funding idleness breaks down families and, ultimately, society. Don't dismiss this out of hand. It is the root of this problem.

We ought to encourage self reliance and self determination in people. Why is it that we have gone away from the rugged individualism that made this country the greatest nation on earth and have replaced it with a nanny state? Are we really that stupid that we need labels on the bottoms of bottles that say "open other end"? Or do we really need warning labels on irons that say "Do not iron clothes on body?" We have created a society of sue happy people who look for every chance to make quick buck for silly and frivolous things and it has encouraged the nanny state. The result is that people cannot buy certain foods, use certain products, take certain medicines, own certain cars, etc. because some part of the bureaucracy has found potential fault. And by definition that also means the curtailing of individual freedom.

Why is it that people can chose to live on a welfare state of entitlements? How is that a legitimate lifestyle choice? We have created a system that makes it better for people to live on welfare than to work a decent job. This is not only wrong, but it is immoral. Recently, Gary Alexander, Secretary of Public Welfare, Commonwealth of Pennsylvania said that because of the generous entitlement system and punitive taxation a "...single mom is better off earning a gross income of $29,000 with

$57,327 in net income and benefits than to a earn gross income of $69,000 with net income and benefits of $57,045." This is not some made up conservative talking point. What this means is that a person earning $69,0000 is living the same way as a person earning only $29,000 because the difference is made up by entitlements. So why work to earn that extra $40,000 if the state will pay you to sit home and watch TV?

This country is slowly creating an unsustainable society of people who want everything and contribute relatively little. We are looking for no risk in life and cradle to grave benefits. A people who think the government can provide all their needs. But what they fail to understand is that the government is not a producer of *anything*. It takes people who must work to grow your food, to make your clothes, to build your home, to manufacture that car or bus, to give you that free vaccination, etc. It isn't coming from the government. It's coming from someone who made it and it is being paid for by someone who worked to earn the money the government took in order to give it to you for free. The government took it from you to give it to someone else. And whatever it couldn't take, it borrowed from nations like China which are ultimately hostile to our future best interests.

Let's frame it differently for the sake of understanding this better. Let's say you were a farmer and your tax liability was $5000 a year. Imagine one morning you woke up and saw people out in your field picking corn. If the value of that corn is about six ears for a dollar, you have someone taking 30,000 ears of corn from the field. That is what the tax liability looks like. What if you earned $1000 a week? Imagine working a week, hard sweat (maybe on a road crew or as a plumber). Friday comes and the boss says "No paycheck for you. This is your taxes." You work another week, same thing. For five Fridays you get no paycheck. That is what this looks like.

We need a revival of that rugged individualism that tamed the West, that built the cities, that promoted the Industrial Revolution, that made living in the USA the envy of the world. We need to get government out of working people's paychecks and to return the welfare system to those only truly in need. Working people have their *own* families to support. They can't be burdened to support those who want to stay home and watch Maury Pauvich or play video games.

We must also get the courts back to sanity. There should be a real and appreciable loss when someone sues--not some contrived punitive damage lottery that creates instant millionaires at the expense of unsuspecting businesses. We need serious tort reform laws and honest recompense for injury or loss instead of looking to strike it rich.

We need to return government to the Constitution and Bill of Rights. What's to say about this that isn't already obvious? As long as our politicians find way to circumvent the checks and balances, the constitional protections, and the limitations placed upon them by the Constitution and the Bill of Rights we will have a chaotic state of affairs.

-People will be arbitrarily arrested and tried unfairly.
-Every aspect of your life will be under surveillance by often unseen eyes and your privacy will no longer exist.
-Police will be able to enter your home and search you and your belongings without a warrant.
-You will need government sanctioned papers to engage in the most basic freedoms--work, travel, build your home, have children, defend your life, raise food, etc.
-Every aspect of your life will be controlled.
-You will never truly own your property and it will always be under threat of seizure.

That list can easily grow. If you think about each of the items above, can it not be said that current government at all levels has "...a history of repeated injuries and usurpations, all having in direct object the establishment of an absolute Tyranny over..." its citizens? That's the language that the Declaration of Independence used against Great Britain. And, worse yet, if you read over the grievances that were listed there, many of them are the same today!

As a proud American, I find that the country I love has been taken over by special interests, oligarchs, plutocrats, Republicans, and Democrats--NONE of which are serving the interests of the people because in embracing one group they are excluding another. This nation was *never* meant to be a Democracy where the mob rules. That form of "majority rules" was specifically rejected by our Founders for what we have today--a Constitutional Republic. And, to the extent that we held onto it, that form of government has served the people well. But today, we have all but rejected it and have exchanged the ideals of Liberty they gave us for the very chains they fought a Revolution to break.

Now, more than ever, we need to return government to the Constitution and Bill of Rights. All of the people's civil liberties must be respected. We have slowly seen the erosion of our civil liberties in every arena of life. If you go down the list, we find that the freedom of speech has been greatly curtailed. People who use the language of liberty are often seen as potential terrorists or flying the Gadsden Flag is somehow considered radical and anti-government. People cannot say Jesus or God in the public arena without being told they are violating some twisted version of the "separation of church and state."

Along those same lines, the freedom *of* religion has become a freedom *from* religion. The classic example is Christmas, where atheists have decided to exclude themselves from the public square during that holiday, but then take the extraordinary step of a fascist insistence that the state enforce the exclusion of any religious displays. This amounts to the state endorsement of atheism or secularism. Anyone who does even a cursory reading of the Founders will see that their lives--both publicly and privately--were filled with open religious expression. No matter how forcefully and loudly the atheists argue their case, the first amendment was *never* meant to exclude religious expression from the public arena.

The press, which was supposed to be free, has instead become the instrument of political propaganda. For example, they failed the American people by not more closely examining the evidence for going to war with Iraq. They have often overlooked politicians' faults when they agreed with their point of view while torturing other politicians whose opinions they reject. Still more, they have neglected significant and newsworthy events. Recent examples include how the Tea Party movement was spoken of by the press with disdain, the Ron Paul presidential candidacy in

2012 was neglected, yet the liberal embrace of the so-called "Occupy Movement" neglected to report many of its short-comings and radicalism. The press greatly favored Hillary Clinton over Donald Trump in 2016 and after Trump won, they have done everything in their power to delegitimize his presidency and to create false scandals by a constant stream of fake news, allegations, insinuations and innuendos.

Add to this that the second amendment is no longer a real right. Citizens must apply to get the right to keep and bear arms. In many states, keeping arms is only by state permission and actually bearing them is even more difficult. If it would seem preposterous to apply for a permit to speak freely or to attend worship services, why does it not seem equally preposterous to need permission to own a gun? Self defense goes with the right to life and liberty. To infringe upon the second amendment is to infringe upon the right to both life and liberty. Criminals want a disarmed public. But the right to life itself has been politicized by abortion and anti-gun rights. The defense of life is somehow seen as illiberal.

This infringement of the Second Amendment hasn't gone unnoticed by the high courts. When the Supreme Court refused to hear a Second Amendment case in June 2017, that decision precipitated this most eloquent dissent from Justice Clarence Thomas (called Peruta v. California)...

"The Court's decision to deny certiorari in this case reflects a distressing trend: the treatment of the Second Amendment as a disfavored right...The Constitution does not rank certain rights above others, and I do not think this Court should impose such a hierarchy by selectively enforcing its preferred rights...
For those of us who work in marbled halls, guarded constantly by a vigilant and dedicated police force, the guarantees of the Second Amendment might seem antiquated and superfluous. But the Framers made a clear choice: They reserved to all Americans the right to bear arms for self-defense. I do not think we should stand by idly while a State denies its citizens that right, particularly when their very lives may depend on it. I respectfully dissent."

The government has also been actively violating the fourth amendment. We have no right to privacy any more. Search and seizure at the hands of government has become commonplace. They have made laws which gives them the right to seize lawful property at will. Local governments have been emboldened by creating a system that puts one's home in jeopardy when he loses his ability to pay real estate tax either by illness or loss of employment. Various federal agencies have arbitrarily confiscated things that they deem illegal in times past, be it gold coins, certain foods, certain intoxicants, embargoed cigars, various imports, etc. A free society cannot have property taken on the whim of legislators. A free society ought to have security in its property.

And the privacy we thought we had is virtually gone. The fourth amendment text reads:

"The right of the people to be secure in their persons, houses, papers, and effects, against unreasonable searches and seizures, shall not be violated, and no warrants shall issue, but upon probable cause, supported by oath or affirmation, and particularly describing the place to be searched, and the persons or things to be seized."

Yet, warrants are no longer required under certain provisions of the USA Patriot Act. Cameras have become ubiquitous in our country, appearing at many intersections and on the streets of many cities. Federal agents can view your email, snail mail, every document about you or by you. They collect phone calls and phone data for every call in the country and around the world. We truly live in a time where there are no secrets. Between Facebook, Instagram, GPS and cell phones, your entire life is now captured and reviewable. The telescreen in George Orwell's dystopian novel "1984" is your cell phone. Unless you remove the battery, it is listening passively to your conversations, the ambient noise around you, the music and TV you hear, all while sitting in your pocket. Whatever you hear, it hears.

I can continue to write on the violations to our civil liberties, but the basic idea is that they have been substantially abrogated by the slow creep of government and this should concern us. For your children's and grandchildren's future, it should concern us!

215

# Conclusion

For those of us who name Jesus as our Lord and Savior, there is an expectation that we speak out against the wrongs going on around us. Jesus was not passive when it came to these issues and neither should we be passive. In some of Jesus' toughest words, He pronounced what could be termed as a screed against those who were the government during His day. This screed is found in Matthew 23 where Jesus throws the book at the Scribes and Pharisees, calling them hypocrites over and over.

Israel had four overlapping levels of government during Jesus' lifetime. There was the imperial government of Rome which could be likened to the federal government. Jesus seldom spoke concerning that government because for the most part they didn't affect the daily lives of the people. Pay them their taxes (i.e. as in Matthew 22:21 when He said "Render unto Caesar the things that are Caesar's") and they will leave you alone was pretty much the extent of His teaching concerning them.

There was also the Herodian Tetrarchy which had a sect of Jews known as Herodians as followers and political adherents. They were Hellenized Jews who often challenged Jesus. These were viewed by Jesus as dishonest and hypocritical in the same ways that the

Pharisees were (cf. Matthew 22:16; Mark 3:6; 8:15; 12:13). Jesus was not shy about calling Herod a "fox" (Luke 13:31-32) which would be considered derogatory and imply that he was not trustworthy. The Herodians were not considered to be a religious party in the same way that the Pharisees and Sadducees were. Their loyalties (as implied by their name) was to politics and the establishment of Herod as their king. They did this because they wanted a theocratic king similar to David or Solomon to rule over them as opposed to an emperor like Caesar. The Herod line were Jewish coverts and seen as friendly to Judaism and a theocracy.

Then there was the governorship of Pontius Pilate which was seen as the Roman side of the equation. It would appear that Herod and Pilate had similar authority. Besides Pilate's part on Jesus' trial and crucifixion, there is no mention of Him during the life and ministry of Jesus. In both cases, Herod's and Pilate's authority seemed to be more about law and order than anything else. Insofar as the daily life of a Jew, they seldom crossed paths.

Finally there were the Scribes, Pharisees, Sadducees, chief priests, elders and the Sanhedrin. These were the chief provocateurs of Jesus in the New Testament. These were the ones about which Jesus had the most to say because it was their laws, rules, policies, regulations and statutes affected the average person's life on a daily basis. And Jesus was not shy about calling them to task for their picayune and statutory oppression. It was because these brought the burden of their rules upon the people that Jesus found the most fault with them. They were the primary face of government in that time. They were the one's who regulated your behavior, who regulated the way you could live, who judged your actions according to their faulty view of the Old Testament law, who added layers of interpretation to that law—often creating contradictions which Jesus pointed out. But instead of enjoying a dynamic and living relationship with God who gave them life, they caused the people to view God as despotic and using fear and compulsion to micromanage every aspect of their lives.

In Jesus' final days, He let these leaders have it. As mentioned earlier, Matthew 23 contains a screed against them. I will end this book with the 20 verses (vv 13-33) in which Jesus gave them a scathing indictment. I believe that Christians should follow Jesus' example and call to task our own government leaders for their oppressions of the people, our neighbors, whom we ought to love as our own selves.

13 "But woe to you, scribes and Pharisees, hypocrites, because you shut off the kingdom of heaven from people; for you do not enter in yourselves, nor do you allow those who are entering to go in.

14 "Woe to you, scribes and Pharisees, hypocrites, because you devour widows' houses, and for a pretense you make long prayers; therefore you will receive greater condemnation.

15 "Woe to you, scribes and Pharisees, hypocrites, because you travel around on sea and land to make one proselyte; and when he becomes one, you make him twice as much a son of hell as yourselves.

16 "Woe to you, blind guides, who say, 'Whoever swears by the temple, that is nothing; but whoever swears by the gold of the temple is obligated.' 17 "You fools and blind men! Which is more important, the gold or the temple that sanctified the gold? 18 "And, 'Whoever swears by the altar, that is nothing, but whoever swears by the offering on it, he is obligated.' 19 "You blind men, which is more important, the offering, or the altar that sanctifies the offering? 20 "Therefore, whoever swears by the altar, swears both by the altar and by everything on it. 21 "And whoever swears by the temple, swears both by the temple and by Him who dwells within it. 22 "And whoever swears by heaven, swears both by the throne of God and by Him who sits upon it.

23 "Woe to you, scribes and Pharisees, hypocrites! For you tithe mint and dill and cummin, and have neglected the weightier

provisions of the law: justice and mercy and faithfulness; but these are the things you should have done without neglecting the others. 24 "You blind guides, who strain out a gnat and swallow a camel!

25 "Woe to you, scribes and Pharisees, hypocrites! For you clean the outside of the cup and of the dish, but inside they are full of robbery and self-indulgence. 26 "You blind Pharisee, first clean the inside of the cup and of the dish, so that the outside of it may become clean also.

27 "Woe to you, scribes and Pharisees, hypocrites! For you are like whitewashed tombs which on the outside appear beautiful, but inside they are full of dead men's bones and all uncleanness. 28 "So you, too, outwardly appear righteous to men, but inwardly you are full of hypocrisy and lawlessness.

29 "Woe to you, scribes and Pharisees, hypocrites! For you build the tombs of the prophets and adorn the monuments of the righteous, 30 and say, 'If we had been living in the days of our fathers, we would not have been partners with them in shedding the blood of the prophets.' 31 "So you testify against yourselves, that you are sons of those who murdered the prophets. 32 "Fill up, then, the measure of the guilt of your fathers. 33 "You

serpents, you brood of vipers, how will you escape the sentence of hell?

Amen

www.ingramcontent.com/pod-product-compliance
Lightning Source LLC
Chambersburg PA
CBHW050907260726
48660CB00001B/77